PERGAMON INTERNATIONAL LIBRARY
of Science, Technology, Engineering and Social Studies
*The 1000-volume original paperback library in aid of education,
industrial training and the enjoyment of leisure*

How to Find Out About
THE SOCIAL SCIENCES

LIBRARY AND TECHNICAL INFORMATION

How to Find Out – A series of guides to international sources of information

GENERAL EDITOR: G. CHANDLER

BAKEWELL, K. G. B.
How to Find Out: Management and Productivity, 2nd edition.

BATE, J.
How to Find Out about Shakespeare

BORCHARDT, D. H.
How to Find Out in Philosophy and Psychology

BURGESS, N.
How to Find Out about Banking and Investment

BURRINGTON, G.
How to Find Out about Statistics

CHANDLER, G.
How to Find Out, 4th edition

CHANDLER, G.
How to Find Out about Literature

MADDEN, L.
How to Find Out about the Victorian Period

PARSONS, S. A. J.
How to Find Out about Economics

ELLIS, A.
How to Find Out about Children's Literature 3rd edition.

FOSKETT, D. J.
How to Find Out in Educational Research

HEPWORTH, P.
How to Find Out in History.

The terms of our inspection copy service apply to all the above books. A complete catalogue of all books in the Pergamon International Library is available on request.

The Publisher will be pleased to receive suggestions for revised editions and new titles.

How to Find Out About
The Social Sciences

by

GILLIAN A. BURRINGTON, FLA
Lecturer, Department of Librarianship, Manchester Polytechnic

PERGAMON PRESS
Oxford · New York · Toronto
Sydney · Paris · Braunschweig

Pergamon Press Offices:

U. K.	Pergamon Press Ltd., Headington Hill Hall, Oxford OX3 0BW, England
U. S. A.	Pergamon Press Inc., Maxwell House, Fairview Park, Elmsford, New York 10523, U.S.A.
C A N A D A	Pergamon of Canada, Ltd., 207 Queen's Quay West, Toronto 1, Canada
A U S T R A L I A	Pergamon Press (Aust.) Pty. Ltd., 19a Boundary Street, Rushcutters Bay, N.S.W. 2011, Australia
F R A N C E	Pergamon Press SARL, 24 rue des Ecoles, 75240 Paris, Cedex 05, France
W E S T G E R M A N Y	Pergamon Press GmbH, 3300 Braunschweig, Postfach 2923, Burgplatz 1, West Germany

First edition 1975

Library of Congress Cataloging in Publication Data

Burrington, Gillian A.
How to find out about the social sciences.

(Library and technical information)
Includes index.
1. Social sciences – Information services – Great
Britain. I. Title.
H62.5.G7B87 1975   300'.7   75-5809
ISBN 0-08-018289-5

Printed in Great Britain by A. Wheaton & Co. Exeter.

Contents

v

List of Illustrations

Preface

The aim of this work is to indicate the sources of information in the social sciences as they are traditionally taught in social science faculties of the universities. There has been no attempt to list all titles of potential use to students, social scientists, or librarians; a work doing this would rapidly become out of date. Rather, the intention has been to show the value of the different types of materials, to describe the scope and use of some of the more significant tools, and to indicate where detailed information on particular subjects can be found.

My thanks go to the staffs of the libraries of Manchester University, the Manchester Business School, · Manchester Polytechnic, the University of Manchester Institute of Science and Technology, the Manchester City Libraries, and the London School of Economics and Political Science, and to the American Economic Association, American Psychological Association, American Political Science Association, American Society for Public Administration, and the American Sociological Association for the help they have given me. I should also like to acknowledge all my students on the Literature and Librarianship of the Social Sciences course at Manchester Polytechnic, with whom I used this material in lectures, and especially Miss Lesley Davies for her help in typing the manuscript and checking bibliographical details. My thanks go also to my husband Douglas for his encouragement and comments.

CHAPTER 1

The Social Sciences: Nature and Scope; Careers; Education and Training

The scope of the social sciences is very much open to debate, but throughout this book it will be regarded in the same way as it is generally regarded in the universities, and in line with that described in *The Social Sciences: an outline for the intending student* (London, Routledge and Kegan Paul, 1965), edited by David C. Marsh, as including sociology, economics, political science, social psychology, and social anthropology. Law, education, history, and linguistics, which are regarded by some as social sciences, are excluded as these subjects are not normally taught within the social sciences faculties of universities. Social administration, about which there is also some debate concerning its validity as a social science, is included in a separate section of the book, as regardless of such arguments it is certainly true that social administrators and social workers are continually drawing on the work of other social scientists, whose findings are constantly influencing ways of solving the social problems of the modern world.

Social science as a respectable academic discipline is really a twentieth-century phenomenon, although people have always been interested in studying their own society, especially in practical areas such as economics and politics, areas which became firmly established as subjects of study long before the other branches of the social sciences. The idea of unified social sciences, despite the claims of such people as Auguste Comte and Herbert Spencer that there could and should be an all-embracing study of all aspects of society, is still very new, and even today many people consider economics, politics, psychology, and anthropology to be distinct disciplines with little interconnection. However, with the growth of interdisciplinary courses in many universities, and with research in all fields of human society becoming increasingly detailed and sophisticated, more scholars are recognizing that

1

they must draw increasingly on the findings of those in other disciplines. Even the economists, whose subject lends itself perhaps more than any other of the social sciences to mathematical techniques, and where research can be kept separate from other branches of the social sciences, cannot totally ignore the findings of the political scientist or the psychologist, and nor can the sociologist ignore information provided by the economist or the anthropologist. These changing attitudes are reflected in the ever-growing wealth of literature and in the nature of recent and current research reports and projects.

The findings of social scientists have had a great impact on society as a whole, and no social administrator or social scientist can fail to be aware of this; indeed, it is partly because of this that the social sciences have achieved respectability. The earliest study to have any real impact on society was Charles Booth's *Labour and Life of the People of London* (London, Macmillan, 1889-1903, 17 vols.), the first social survey, which was undertaken not by an academic, but by a shrewd businessman who became concerned with the problems of unemployment and poverty in London, and carried out the first scientific study in order to find out whether the problem was as great as some people believed. Largely as a result of this and Seebohm Rowntree's survey of York, entitled *Poverty: a study of town life* (London, Macmillan, 1901), several of the social services which are now taken for granted, such as old-age pensions, unemployment and health insurance, and free school meals for those unable to pay, were introduced during the first decade of the century. Both world wars stimulated the study of psychology, economics, and sociology in the field of selection and allocation of people to the tasks for which they were most suited, the development of propaganda and counter-propaganda techniques, rationing and other methods of allocation of scarce resources, and post-war rebuilding, stimulated a number of community surveys to find out what was wanted and needed by people in the towns which were to be rebuilt after the bomb damage. More recently studies have revealed a great deal of information about stress and anxiety caused by high rise and high density housing developments, and as a direct result of these findings many local authorities which have hitherto been committed to such developments have modified their plans. Knowledge gained by sociologists and psychologists is slowly changing attitudes to and treatment of certain types of offenders, as well as attitudes to the mentally handicapped. Many specialist pressure groups have grown up with the aim of making society aware of the problems of the disadvantaged, and such groups rely to a great extent on the findings of the academic social scientists.

CAREERS

The range of careers open to social scientists is almost unending, with openings in industry, economic and market research, personnel or general management, the civil service and local government, as well as in a variety of welfare services, although many such careers need a professional qualification as well as a social science degree.

There are several guides to careers available in Britain and the United States. General guides, while not giving very much detail about the careers which they describe, are useful in the initial stages of career selection, and they usually give details of specialist publications which can be consulted. Some of the more useful ones are listed below:

CENTRAL YOUTH EMPLOYMENT EXECUTIVE. *Opportunity in the Professions, Industry and Commerce* (London, HMSO). Covers some eighty careers, and gives information about the nature of work involved, pre-entry requirements, training, and prospects.

DENT, H. C. *Yearbook of Technical Education and Careers in Industry* (London, Black). This is a useful guide because as well as describing the careers and opportunities it gives extensive coverage of courses, specialist organizations, and government and industrial training schemes.

EDMONDS, P. J. *Careers Encyclopaedia: a work of reference upon some 220 occupations . . .* (London, Macmillan). Issued every two years, this work gives very thorough coverage of career opportunities in Britain and the possible methods of entering the various professions, together with the entry qualifications required.

HOPKE, W. E. *Encyclopaedia of Careers and Vocational Guidance* (New York, Doubleday). The first volume of this work is devoted to planning careers and acquiring the necessary qualifications; the second is concerned with work and prospects in individual occupations. It is the most comprehensive guide for the United States.

PETERSON, C. E. *Careers for College Graduates: selection, preparation, attainment and advancement* (New York, Barnes & Noble).

UNITED STATES DEPARTMENT OF LABOR. *Occupational Outlook Handbook* (Washington, US Government Printing Office).

UNIVERSITY OF LONDON. Appointments Board. *Careers for Graduates* (London, Oxford University Press).

More specific guides are issued to individual careers, many by the professional associations, others by potential employers. These include:

AMERICAN SOCIOLOGICAL ASSOCIATION. *A Career in Sociology* (Washington, ASA).

BRITISH PSYCHOLOGICAL SOCIETY. *Careers in Psychology* (London, BPS).

BRITISH SOCIOLOGICAL ASSOCIATION. *Sociology and Social Anthropology* (London, BSA).

EULAU, H. and MARCH, J. G. *Political Science* (Englewood Cliffs, NJ, Prentice-Hall).

EDUCATION AND TRAINING

In the United Kingdom historical accident has afforded a multiplicity of possible methods of qualifying for almost any career. There are full-time and part-time courses leading to professional qualifications; courses at technical colleges leading to the colleges' own diplomas or to the Higher National Diploma or Certificate; college courses leading to degrees awarded either by the Council for National Academic Awards or by London University and courses at universities leading to either a first or a higher degree, or to a postgraduate diploma which may in some cases be accepted by a professional association as a sufficient qualification or in others as only a pre-entry requirement. In view of the wide range of possibilities, selection of a suitable course can be difficult, especially as many qualifications are of theoretically equal status, as in the case of CNAA degrees and those issued by universities, or the HND that is designated by the Department of Education and Science as a degree equivalent, are not always so judged by prospective employers.

In the United States there is less confusion, as the only means of gaining qualifications is through the universities and colleges.

Details of courses and the qualifications to which they lead can be found in the following:

AMERICAN COUNCIL OF EDUCATION. *American Universities and Colleges* (Washington, The Council). This work gives information on higher and professional education, and lists accredited and approved schools in the field as well as a complete list of accredited colleges and universities with their resources, equipment, entrance requirements, staffing, class size, degrees awarded, and fees.

AMERICAN COUNCIL ON EDUCATION. *Guide to Graduate Study Programs Leading to the PhD Degree* (Washington, The Council).

AMERICAN SOCIOLOGICAL ASSOCIATION. *Guide to Graduate Departments of Sociology* (Washington, ASA).

CAREERS RESEARCH ADVISORY CENTRE. *Graduate Studies* (London.

CRAC). Volume 1 covers the humanities and social sciences, and lists all postgraduate degrees, diplomas, and certificates, as well as giving details of research facilities, content of courses, and profiles of the universities and polytechnics which offer such courses.

CAREERS RESEARCH ADVISORY CENTRE. *Yearbook of Education and Training* (London, CRAC). The work covers all aspects of training and education from GCE O-level upwards.

COMMITTEE OF DIRECTORS OF POLYTECHNICS. *Handbook of Polytechnic Courses* (London, Lund Humphries). This work gives details of the scope and nature of advanced non-degree courses, CNAA degree courses, and HNDs.

COUNCIL FOR NATIONAL ACADEMIC AWARDS. *Compendium of Degree Courses* (London, CNAA). Lists special features of each course.

Directory of Further Education (London, Cornmarket). This volume is primarily concerned with polytechnics and other colleges, with emphasis on awards issued by the CNAA, college diplomas, HNC, and professional •qualifications.

REGIONAL ADVISORY COUNCILS IN ENGLAND AND WALES. *Compendium of Advanced Courses in Technical Colleges* (London, The Council).

Which University? (London, Cornmarket). The first section is a subject companion to courses; the second is devoted to the universities, describing academic life, student life, amenities, and special features.

FINDING EMPLOYMENT

The newly qualified social scientist will almost undoubtedly make use of the services offered by appointments boards in universities and colleges. These boards are given details of vacancies and openings for those with qualifications in a particular subject area, and many arrange for potential employers to hold interviews during the students' final year. This can be particularly useful for those who at this stage are still unsure of where they would like to pursue a career. Many potential employers also advertise their openings in guides which are available in the appointments boards, and which give details of what degree subjects would be suitable qualifications for a career in a particular organization. These guides include:

CAREERS RESEARCH ADVISORY CENTRE. *Careers Beyond a Degree: a comprehensive guide to graduate employment, employers recruiting graduates and post-graduate study* (London, CRAC, issued annually).

Directory of Opportunities for Graduates (London, Cornmarket, issued annually). This guide includes a careers advice section and has a useful degree subject index.

Graduate Opportunities (London, New Opportunities Press, issued annually).

Newspaper advertisements are another source of information about employment opportunities. Most serious daily and weekly newspapers carry advertisements for posts ranging from relatively junior to senior executive levels, and some journals are devoted to advertisements for jobs, as, for example, *Appointments Magazine* (London, Brittain Press, issued bi-weekly), which covers all subject fields.

A journal devoted to a particular subject can be another useful source of information, especially if it appears at frequent intervals: those which are only issued quarterly are of very limited value for this purpose, except occasionally for some senior level post. Other useful sources include *New Society* (London, New Science Publications, issued weekly), which specializes in advertisements in social administration and social work; *News and Views* (Washington, American Society for Public Administration, issued monthly); and *American Sociologist* (Washington, American Sociological Association, issued monthly).

Placement services are another means of finding employment. In the United Kingdom the Department of Employment and Productivity maintains a professional and executive register of some 22,000 people. Whenever an employer notifies a vacancy, details of suitably qualified candidates are given to him. There are also several commercial placement services, such as Management Selection, 17 Stratton Street, London, W1, and Graduate and Professional Careers Register, 42 Conduit Street, London, W1. Such agencies frequently advertise in newspapers and periodicals. In the United States there are over 5000 employment agencies and placement bureaux, as well as the United States Employment Service which operates at State and national levels. A useful guide to such services is the *National Directory of Employment Services* (Detroit, Mich., Gale, 1962), which lists university placement bureaux and specialized services operated by individual appointments boards as well as those operated by professional associations such as the American Economic Association and the American Sociological Association, and the private employment agencies.

CHAPTER 2

Libraries

VALUE OF LIBRARIES

Because their bibliographical needs are so wide, and because they need material on such a wide range of subjects, social scientists will inevitably find themselves using not just one library, but several. Almost all printed materials are of potential value, and it is useful if social scientists are aware of the kinds of library which are most likely to be able to satisfy their needs as well as of the kinds of service which they offer.

GUIDES TO THE USE OF LIBRARIES

There are several books which explain in general terms how to make the best use of libraries. These include *How to Find Out*, by G. Chandler (Oxford, Pergamon Press, 3rd edn., 1967); *Books and Libraries*, by R. O. Linden (London, Cassel, 1965); and *Using Libraries*, by Kenneth Whittaker (London, Deutsch, 3rd edn., 1972). These cover such topics as general bibliographical services, types of material (such as encyclopedias and periodicals), arrangement of libraries, and the services they are most likely to offer. Another useful work is *Guide to the Use of Books and Libraries*, by U. K. Gates (New York, McGraw-Hill, 2nd edn., 1969), which deals specifically with college libraries, describing various kinds of material and their organization.

Many individual libraries, especially the large public and academic ones, issue guides to their own collections and services. These are particularly useful because not only do they give the obvious information about where subjects are located, thereby often saving time for the newcomer, but they also draw attention to any special materials such as manuscripts or bequests which are not on general display. Such materials are by no means limited to old or rare publications: many libraries keep the original notebooks relating to a piece of social research, and many a social scientist has left his collection of books on

7

a particular topic to his favourite library. Library guides also frequently list the names and telephone extensions of library staff who specialize in particular subject areas and who will answer bibliographical inquiries.

SPECIAL LIBRARY COLLECTIONS

Although it is possible to obtain almost any material on request from other libraries, it is often more convenient for someone in search of information to visit a library which is likely to be able to satisfy his needs immediately. There is a further advantage in visiting another library rather than requesting that material be borrowed. This is that it is often difficult, and sometimes impossible, to assess from the title of a work alone how useful it is going to be. Social scientists stand to gain much from browsing as, unlike in the relatively well-defined fields of science and technology, the social sciences are only vaguely delineated and, because of the nature of the subject, abstracts are usually what librarians describe as indicative rather than informative (see Chapter 5). Even a student may find it sometimes necessary to use the resources of the local public library as well as those of the university or college. At a later stage in his career he may also need to use the libraries of other large or specialist organizations, or of government departments, especially if he is pursuing research.

In Britain the most comprehensive stock of primary social science materials, the source materials for much academic research, is held by the British Library (BL) Reference Division, formerly called the British Museum Library. This library is, one hopes, in the not too distant future to be rehoused; and with the increased seating space then available the current problem of gaining access to this wealth of material will be reduced. Apart from its British book, journal, and newspaper stock, which is based on the material it acquires from its status as the major legal deposit library in the United Kingdom, it also spends some £100,000 each year on foreign material, much of which is not available elsewhere in the country. Perhaps most important of all for social scientists, and for social and economic historians in particular, is the collection of printed ephemera, including election manifestoes; reports of political parties, trade unions, learned societies, and professional associations; advertising literature; house magazines (the journals of business organizations which are produced for their own staff); and many purely local publications such as church and school magazines, local society reports, railway and bus timetables. These are invaluable not only for their factual content, but also as aids in assessing the mood of an earlier age.

Unfortunately, many provincial publications, although they do fall within the scope of the laws on deposit, have not been acquired, largely due to the Copyright Office's having been unable to keep pace with the great flow of published and semi-published material.

The main reading room of the BL has 300 seats, usually all occupied, which is in itself an indication of the library's importance as a research centre. Because British books take some nine months to appear in the catalogue, and foreign publications up to two years, it is not suitable for current research. There are also special reading rooms: the State Paper Room, housing official British and foreign publications, which handles most of the bibliographical inquiries; the Electoral Registers Room, which houses all current registers and is heavily used by market researchers; the Newspaper Library, which is housed not at the BL itself, but at Colindale, a short journey away, and which holds not only all British newspapers but also representative foreign ones. National libraries of other countries are similarly rich in this kind of source material.

The BL (Lending Division), housed at Boston Spa in Yorkshire, has been formed by the amalgamation of the National Lending Library for Science and Technology and the National Central Library. The former began purchasing social science serial publications in 1966, and acquired what was probably the most comprehensive loan collection in the country of recent journals, conference proceedings, reports, as well as British and American doctoral theses, in the social sciences. The book stock of the latter was extensive in the social sciences and humanities from both Britain and abroad. The merger of these two libraries makes a most impressive collection, and requests for material are usually satisfied within a few days.

The major academic library for social scientists in Britain is the British Library of Political and Economic Science (BLPES) at the London School of Economics (Houghton Street, Aldwych, London WC2). This library was founded in 1896, largely owing to the enthusiasm of Sydney Webb, and although it is the working library of the London School of Economics its services are available to all researchers, as much of its material is not available for consultation elsewhere. Despite its title, the scope of the BLPES is of the social sciences as a whole, and includes transport, public administration, law, sociology, all aspects of history, philosophy, psychology, mathematics, and linguistics, as well as economics, business administration, statistics, and political science, not only in the English language but also in the major European ones. It has a large number of government publications from all over the world, and is a depository for federal publications of the United

States and for United Nations publications. It holds a unique collection of local authority reports as well as collections of reports from banks, railways, and other official bodies. Of immense research value are the manuscript collections of diaries and working papers of people notable in the world of scholarship and public affairs, such as Tawney, Malinowski, G. B. Shaw, Violet Markham, Lord Dalton, Lord Beveridge, Ramsey McDonald, and Charles Booth. Apart from its own collections in this field, the BLPES has published a survey of hitherto unpublished data relevant to the social sciences and available in libraries of government departments, and in 1972 received a further grant from the Social Science Research Council to locate other papers of people and bodies active in British politics from 1901 to 1951.

There are two useful guides to libraries in the United Kingdom. *The Libraries Museums and Art Galleries Yearbook* (London, Clarke) is arranged in two main sections – public and special libraries, each subdivided according to location, with a subject index. It gives details of any special collections maintained by the library. The *Aslib Directory* (London, Aslib, 3rd edn., 1968, 2 vols.) is useful for the comprehensiveness of each entry, and also for its very detailed subject index.

Almost all countries possess outstanding national and university libraries: the Bibliothèque Nationale in France; the Deutsche Bücherei and the Staatsbibliothek in East Germany; the Library of Congress, Yale and Harvard universities in America, all of which have impressive collections of materials relating to their country's growth and development. There are a number of directories in this area such as *Subject Collections in European Libraries: a directory and bibliographical guide,* by R. C. Lewanski (New York, Bowker, 1965). France is covered by *Repertoire des Bibliothèques d'Étude et Organismes de Documentation* (Paris, Bibliothèque Nationale, 1963). For Austria there is *Handbuch der österreichischen Bibliotheken* (Vienna, Österreichische Nationalbibliothek, 1961-3, 3 vols.) and for West and East Germany respectively there is *Jahrbuch der deutschen Bibliotheken* (Wiesbaden, Harrasowitz) and *Jahrbuch der Bibliotheken* (Berlin, Archiv und Dokumentationsstellen der DDR). The *American Library Directory* (New York, Bowker, 28th edn., 1972, revised biennially) gives details of some 20,000 libraries in the United States and Canada and is usefully supplemented by *Subject Collections: a guide to special book collections and subject emphasis as reported by university, college, public and special libraries in the United States and Canada* (New York, Bowker, 3rd edn., 1967). Other useful guides include *The Directory of Special Libraries and Information Centers,* edited by A. T. Kruzas (Detroit, Gale Research Company, 3rd edn., 1970), which consists of an alphabetical list of libraries with a detailed subject index. However, the practice of referring to libraries by number, which gives rise to long lists of numbers after each subject heading, makes it cumbersome in use. The *Directory of Information Resources in the United States* (Washington, National Referral Center for Science and Technology, Library of Congress, 1966-7, 4 vols.) also lists a great many organizations providing information in the social sciences, even in cases where only small library services are furnished.

LIBRARY SERVICES

Inter-library Co-operation

Just as it is impossible for any individual to possess all the printed material he might need, so too is it impossible for any library to contain every item which might be needed by users. Even the great national libraries such as the Library of Congress and the Bibliothèque Nationale cannot have all the books required by their readers in their own country, as researchers — especially in the social sciences — naturally want material published abroad. And even where there is a strong tradition of adding foreign material to stock, there is no guarantee that this is what will be required. Therefore librarians have for many years organized schemes for inter-lending by which they agree, in return for being able to borrow books from other libraries, also to lend them on request. In Great Britain, for example, every public library, as well as some special libraries, is linked through the Regional Library Bureaux to the BL (Lending Division). Any request for a book not held by the library where it is received, and not due to be purchased, will be circulated throughout the whole country, and abroad if necessary, until a library is found which is prepared to lend its copy. There are similar schemes operating between special and academic libraries. Inter-library lending schemes are not limited to the United Kingdom. Similar arrangements exist in almost all countries and the majority participate in international lending.

The advantage of schemes such as these is that the researcher's ability to obtain copies of items which may no longer be in print is considerably enhanced. The social scientist in particular, unlike his technological counterpart, needs older material; and in many cases, even where the material may be available through commercial channels, the librarian might not feel justified in buying it for his own library's stock because it could be expensive and little used.

Photocopying

Many libraries have a photocopying service which is available to users. The law forbids one person copying the whole of a publication or making more than one copy of any part of it, but it can often be very useful to make an instantaneous copy of a page whose information cannot be quickly and readily digested.

Photocopies are frequently used for inter-library loan purposes, as it is much cheaper to send the photocopy of an article through the post than to send the whole issue of the journal from which it is taken, or even the whole year's issues if they have been bound together. The cost of copying is usually passed on to the reader, but he then has the advantage of a permanent record. The one disadvantage of this method for social scientists is that often it is difficult, if not impossible, to assess how useful an article is going to prove until it has been read, and many an apparently hopeful title proves fruitless. A student on a limited grant will not be very enthusiastic at being charged for something which he will immediately discard, and he should therefore be wary of sending indiscriminately for every possibly useful article.

Bibliographical Services

It is becoming increasingly common for academic libraries to serve their readers in a number of ways which are different from the more traditional notion of conservation of stock. It is now possible in many libraries to ask for bibliographies to be compiled on particular subjects. Such bibliographies are undoubtedly of value to both teacher and researcher, and to the latter especially if they are extended to include items which are not available in the compiling library's stock, which may not be strong in all areas. Whilst they cannot replace the work which the researcher must do, they can nevertheless be very valuable.

Library Instruction

Nearly all academic libraries give some instruction in the use of the catalogue, carrying out a literature search, and using certain kinds of bibliographical materials. These are generally given to groups of undergraduates or research students at the beginning of their course. Despite appearances, it is worth while attending such instruction, which may vary from an hour, when it will be a basic introduction to the library and the services it gives, to several hours spread over perhaps a term. Librarians usually welcome members of the academic staff attending these courses, which are naturally directed at particular subjects.

Current Awareness Services

This is another relatively new field into which academic libraries are expanding. At their simplest these services consist of a weekly or fortnightly bulletin listing new books which have been added to stock, usually arranged in broad subject groupings, by faculty or by department, thereby overcoming the tendency of the classification to separate subjects which might well be used together. There are several variations on this method. Some libraries notify individual departments of new material which is of interest to them, but the disadvantage of this is that not everyone is going to see the bulletin, especially if only one copy is sent, and students who might find such a list useful are unlikely to see it at all. Other libraries produce photocopies of the contents pages of current journals, distribute them to departments, or make them available for consultation in the library, whilst others provide similar services but take each area in turn so that the interests of every department or faculty are covered thoroughly at intervals of a term or so.

Selective Dissemination of Information Services

A few academic libraries have recently been experimenting with providing selective dissemination of information services, whereby individual users are informed of material which might be of value to their specific needs. There are immense problems in provision of such services in the social sciences because not only is the identification of a user's needs difficult, as he himself is often unaware of how useful a particular item may be until he has seen it, but also because there is relatively little hard literature in the subject. Also, because of the lack of uniformity in social science terminology between one subject and another (and between one author and another in the same subject), it is difficult to use computers in literature searching. The difficulties are further increased because the possible input of documents is enormous; almost everything is potentially of use to some social scientist. Nevertheless, some academic libraries are providing such services, and they have so far been well received by their clientele, especially as in most cases the librarians who are in charge of the services were themselves social science graduates.

Cutting Files

Most public libraries maintain files of newspaper cuttings on all topics, which can be of great value to researchers as they are usually taken out not only from the "quality" papers but also from local and other newspapers which the library may receive but not file permanently. Such files usually contain biographical information as well as reports on important political and other events. Sadly, too few library users realize that such sources exist and are so readily available, and therefore they tend to be very much under used.

Company Information and Advertising Material

The larger public libraries which have separate commerical departments frequently have files of company information and advertising material which is sent to them as a matter of course. Mostly this is used by economic historians, but other social scientists can also find it useful. The main problem for users is that frequently the material is arranged only in alphabetical order by name of company, and unless there is a good indexing system it is difficult to ensure adequate search coverage on a specific topic. A further problem is that many libraries dispose of this material after a few years, whilst it is only after the passage of time that it is likely to be of value to anyone with an historical interest.

Reserve Collections

Reserve collections are those which for some reason — usually they are older or little used books — are not on general display, but must be housed elsewhere owing to restrictions on space, sometimes even in another building or at another site. Clearly the disadvantage here is that it is impossible for most readers to go and browse among the wealth of material housed in these collections; however, occasionally users are allowed to search such stocks if they are considered to be engaged in serious research.

Microfilm Collections

Because of the ever-present problems of space more and more little used material is being stored on microfilm (a continuous roll of film transparency) or on microfiche (a card transparency). By these means complete runs of newspapers and journals can be stored in a very limited space, and today more and more limited circulation publications such as reports are being produced in this way. As with photocopies, it is considerably cheaper to send material through the post, especially to foreign countries, if it is in microform, and all American doctoral dissertations are now reproduced in this way. Useful as microforms undoubtedly are, they present problems, the most significant of which is that they must be used in conjunction with special equipment, called readers, in order to make them legible. This means that they can only be consulted in the library, which is not always convenient for the researcher.

Local History Collections

These are found in public libraries and can provide a wealth of valuable information for social and economic historians. They usually contain complete runs of local newspapers, local authority reports, local publications such as school magazines and society newsletters, together with photographs of the changing locality, local maps, electoral registers, and a wealth of other materials which can be of use not only for their original purpose, and are the source materials of the social scientist when he is studying a community.

ARRANGEMENT OF LIBRARIES

Classification

The purpose of classification in libraries is to ensure that all books on the same subject are brought together in one place and that related subjects are side by side. Unfortunately it is less easy to do this than might be expected, as most subject specialists have different ideas as to what is the most suitable arrangement for their subject or which subjects are most closely related to their own. It is because of this lack of general consensus that there are several classification schemes in existence, each trying to satisfy the requirements of library users.

The scheme most widely used in public libraries, and which is also used in many academic libraries is the Dewey Decimal Classification (DC) which was first published in 1876 and is now in its 18th edition, each edition subtly changing and expanding to allow for growing and changing knowledge. A variant and descendant of this scheme is the Universal Decimal Classification (UDC), which is used in many university and technical libraries.

DC divides knowledge into ten broad divisions, 000-900, as follows:

000 General works
100 Philosophy, psychology
200 Religion
300 Social Sciences
400 Language
500 Science
600 Technology
700 Arts, recreation
800 Literature
900 History, biography, geography

Each main division is then divided into ten classes, e.g.:

300 Social sciences
310 Statistics
320 Political science
330 Economics
340 Law
350 Administration
360 Social welfare
370 Education
380 Communications
390 Customs

These are then further subdivided into ten subclasses, e.g.:

330 Economics
331 Labour
332 Lucrative capital
333 Land
334 Co-operative systems
335 Collectivist systems and schools
336 Public finance
338 Production
339 Distribution of capital goods and consumption of consumer goods.

After the third digit a decimal point is introduced, e.g.:

338.6 Systems
338.63 Cottage industries
338.64 Small industries
338.65 Large industries

This allows for infinite expansion so that new subjects can be added into the scheme as they arise — and in the most suitable place. Unfortunately for subject specialists, particularly in the social sciences, new subjects do not always arise as a further division of another, unlike in technology, where this is normally the case. In the social sciences it is not uncommon for new subjects to be based on two or more different subjects which might be widely spaced in the classification scheme. It is for this reason that some users and some librarians prefer the UDC, which is much more flexible than DC and allows for more combinations of subjects by the use of various signs, the most common of which are the + and the : signs. These are useful and precise, but present problems for users who are often unable to locate material on the shelves because they do not understand the order of the symbols, and thus much of the value of a detailed classification scheme is forfeited.

The Library of Congress Classification (LC) is another scheme which is widely used in academic libraries, and was designed originally to satisfy the needs of the United States National Library in Washington. Subjects are arranged primarily by letters of the alphabet and subdivided by numbers, but not arranged decimally as in DC and UDC, new subjects being catered for by slotting them into spaces which were left where growth was expected. This again has led to some unsatisfactory arrangements as far as subject specialists are concerned, although it should be remembered that it caters for the needs of the Library of Congress very adequately. The scheme is basically arranged as follows:

A General works
B Philosophy, religion
C History, auxiliary sciences
D History and topography (excluding America)
E-F History and topography of America
G Geography
H Social science
J Political science
K Law
L Education
M Music
N Fine arts
P Language and literature
Q Science
R Medicine
S Agriculture
T Technology
U Military science
Z Bibliography

A second letter is then added before the digits are introduced, e.g.:

JC   The state
JC11   General works
JC311 Nationalism
JC329 Patriotism

A newer scheme which has recently been developed specifically with particular social scientists in mind is the London Classification of Business Studies (LCB) which, whilst not covering the whole of the area of the social sciences, nevertheless includes a great deal of it; business cannot work in isolation from the rest of society, and its literature reflects this. The scheme was originally devised for the London Graduate School of Business Studies, and because of its structure is capable of infinite expansion and is highly flexible. It is already being used by other libraries of the same type, and seems to be successful in that it is easy to use, both for the librarian and the reader, and satisfies most people as to arrangement, which is broadly as follows:

A Management
B Marketing
C Production
D Research and development
E Finance
F Personnel
G Office services
J Economics
K Industries
L Behavioural sciences
M Communication
N Education
P Law
R Science and technology
S Philosophy, logic, and scientific method
T Operational research
U Statistics
V Mathematics
W Automation
X Organization and methods and work study

Each of these areas are then further divided by another letter, e.g.:

LA Behavioural sciences
LC Sociology
LE Population studies
LG Social stratification
LX Psychology

From the arrangement of the subjects it can be seen that this scheme will not be satisfactory for all social scientists, but in a library serving economists or management scientists it will clearly be useful, as will the Classification of Business Literature which was originally prepared by the Library of the Harvard University Graduate School of Business Administration, and which is also widely used in management libraries.

Whichever scheme it operates, it is likely that the library will produce some kind of guide to the arrangement, showing any modifications which are in use. This should be studied carefully, as it will save the reader a great deal of time.

Catalogues

There are various physical forms of catalogues in use, the most common being the card catalogue which is filed in drawers in a cabinet. Some catalogues are on loose-leaf sheets held in sheaf binders; others are printed in book form or have slips pasted into books, although these are not commonly used for expanding collections. Today some libraries produce computer-printed catalogues with frequent supplements and new editions to keep them up to date.

There are two main methods of arrangements for a catalogue – the dictionary, which has entries for authors, subjects, and titles in one alphabetical sequence, and the classified, which takes its name from the main sequence, as this follows the order used for arranging the books on the shelves. Whatever the arrangement used, the entries will all give a minimum amount of information – author, title, publication date, and location mark.

Dictionary Catalogue

Because the dictionary catalogue is in one alphabetical sequence, it is often thought that it is easier to use than the classified, but there are two disadvantages. The first and most immediately noticeable is that not all books on the same subject will be brought together, as they are obviously scattered by the alphabet. By contrast, the purpose of the classified catalogue is to bring all entries for one subject to one place. This means that the dictionary catalogue must have references from a general term to all related headings, e.g.:

SOCIOLOGY
See also
CLASS

CULTURE
DEVIANCE
GROUPS
INSTITUTIONS (etc.)

and from terms which are not used to those synonymous ones which are, e.g.:

SOCIAL STRUCTURE
see
CLASS

or from one form of heading to another, e.g.:

HISTORY, SOCIAL
see
SOCIAL HISTORY

The second problem encountered when using the dictionary catalogue is that the filing order can cause confusion. For instance, where the filing word is the same for an author, a title, a subject, or a place, there are rules for the order in which they must appear in the catalogue. An example is the word "Wakefield". Here the generally accepted order is:

Wakefield, John (author)
Wakefield, John (a biography)
Wakefield: Directories (subject)
Wakefield Worthies (title)

Classified Catalogue

The classified catalogue has three parts. The main sequence is filed by the classification mark; and where there are several entries at the same mark, these are arranged alphabetically according to the surnames of the authors. The second part is the name index, which is an alphabetical list of authors, editors, biographers, or any other person likely to be associated with the book, as well as some titles, though titles are not usually recorded in the name index unless they are distinctive and likely to be remembered, or the work is anonymous. The third sequence is the subject index, which is an alphabetical list of subjects together with their classification marks, e.g.:

Class: sociology 301.44
Econometrics: economics 330.018

Equality: political science 323.5
Equality: sociology 301.45
Propaganda: politics 329.01
Socialism: economics 335

(The example uses class marks from the Dewey Decimal Classification.)

When the classification mark has been found it is possible to go directly to the shelves to see what books are immediately available. However, if a serious search is being made, it is preferable to consult the classified sequence. This shows all the material held in the library stock regardless of whether it is on loan or in use, or whether it is in the main shelf sequence or not. Most libraries have at least two shelf sequences, the main one, and one for larger-than-average-height books, and it should not be forgotten that there is usually also a sequence of quick reference books on all subjects. These will be shown in the catalogue by some symbol, usually a prefix, such as QR for reference material. The classified sequence will also indicate entries for books which are shelved at a more general class mark or a related subject. This is particularly useful as so many books are multi- or polytopical, but cannot of course be shelved in more than one place. Such entries will usually have the following format:

942.06
shelved at
301.0942
    BUTTERWORTH, Eric
    The sociology of modern Britain: an introductory reader; edited by
    Eric Butterworth and David Weir. London: Fontana, 1970. 340p

One point to be watched in any catalogue, regardless of its basic arrangement, is its method of filing in the alphabetical sequence. There are two possible methods. One is to include all the letters in all the words of a heading in the alphabetization irrespective of how they are broken up; the other treats each word separately. These methods are known as "letter by letter" and "word by word" (also referred to as "nothing before something") respectively. An example is:

VAN
VANDERBILT   (letter by letter arrangement)
VAN DER POST
and

VAN
VAN DER POST   (word by word arrangement)
VANDERBILT

It should not be forgotten that although the main book catalogue is the one which usually receives most prominence in a library, there are often other catalogues which may be separately housed or may form separate sequences in the main catalogue. These are usually for non-book or special materials, such as theses, microforms, or periodicals. Frequently the material they contain is not classified in the same way as the rest of the stock: periodicals, for example, may be arranged in more broad groups than the books and subdivided by title; theses either by department or author, and the catalogues will usually reflect these differences. Indeed, it is because of these differences that there are usually separate catalogues and all of them are potentially valuable to the researcher in the social sciences, who is likely to find that he uses relatively few books in comparison with other materials.

CHAPTER 3

Organizations

NATIONAL PROFESSIONAL ASSOCIATIONS, LEARNED SOCIETIES, AND RESEARCH ORGANIZATIONS

The distinctions between professional associations, learned societies, and research organizations are not always clear cut, but basically the professional associations are concerned both with the qualified and the qualifying, and in some measure recognize professional competence. The learned societies cater for the needs of specialists, and their membership is usually restricted to those who are already qualified, while the research bodies are primarily concerned with carrying out research and publishing results, although some learned societies and professional associations also do this. The functions fulfilled by these last two types of body are manifold. Most publish information which might not be issued by commercial publishers because it is of restricted interest. Societies issue their publications either as journals or as occasional papers or research reports. Almost all hold meetings or conferences, issuing the proceedings, and have special study groups. Many maintain libraries, or information services, that can often be used by non-members of the organization, while others publish bibliographies, undertake research, often functioning as a pressure group in activating social or economic reform, and some give recognition for professional competence and maintain an employment register.

Details of these types of organization can be found in the following:

CURRIE, Sir James. *Professional Organisations in the Commonwealth* (London, Hutchinson, for the Commonwealth Foundation, 1970), which gives details of the aims of each body with a list of their publications. Although not comprehensive in coverage this is the most useful source of information on such organizations in the Commonwealth.

23

Directory of British Associations (Beckenham, Kent, CBD Research, 3rd edn., 1970). This guide gives concisely codified details about each body, covering aims, membership, activities, publications, information services, and other useful information where applicable. Its coverage of societies in the United Kingdom is more comprehensive than any other publication. A new edition is to be published early in 1974.

Directory of European Associations (Beckenham, Kent, CBD Research). Part 1: *National Industrial Trade and Professional Associations,* 1971. This guide has the same format as the one mentioned above, and like that work is very comprehensive in coverage. Part 2: *Scientific and Learned Societies,* is to appear towards the end of 1975.

Encyclopedia of Associations (Detroit, Mich., Gale, 5th edn., 1968, 2 vols. + supplements) (Fig. 1). This is a broadly classified work with a subject index and an excellent network of cross-references. It gives copious details of the aims, membership, activities, and publications of each association, and its updating supplements appear quarterly.

Yearbook of International Organizations (Brussels, Union of International Associations). This work gives regularly up-dated information on over 4000 bodies.

There is only one work which is devoted entirely to the social sciences:

World Index of Social Science Institutions (Paris, Unesco, 1970). This is a loose-leaf publication, continuously up-dated. The information it gives is brief but adequate, and includes the major publications of each organization.

The following list of learned societies, professional associations, and research bodies is not intended to be comprehensive, but is a guide to the more significant organizations in the major social science areas, as these are the bodies which are most likely to be used at some time by most social scientists. Only brief indications of their activities are given, and full bibliographical details of their journals can be found in Chapter 5.

United Kingdom

ACTON SOCIETY TRUST, 18 Victoria Park Square, London, E 2. Founded 1948. This is a research body concerned with social problems, especially in the field of relationships of individuals to the impersonal forces of modern society. Its findings are published in the form of research reports and occasional papers.

Section 9 - PUBLIC AFFAIRS ORGANIZATIONS

AMERICAN ECONOMIC ASSOCIATION (AEA)
1313 21st Ave. S.   Phone: (615) 322-2595
Nashville, Tenn. 37207
Prof. Rendings Fels, Sec.-Treas.
Founded 1885 - Members 18,259 - Staff 10. Educators, business
executives, government administrators, journalists, lawyers and others
interested in economics and its application to present-day problems.
To encourage historical and statistical research into actual conditions
of industrial life and provide a non-partisan forum for economic discussion. Committees: Economic Education, Research and Publications.
Publications: (1) American Economic Review, quarterly; (2) Journal
of Economic Literature, quarterly; (3) Papers and Proceedings, annual;
(4) Handbook, irregular; (5) Monographs, irregular; (6) Cumulative
Index (11-volume index of all English-language economic journals);
also publishes translations of foreign economic classics. Convention/
Meeting: Annual - 1974 Dec. 28-30, San Francisco, Calif.;
1975 Oct. 2-4, Dallas, Tex.; 1976 Sept. 16-18, Atlantic City,
N.J.; 1977 Dec. 28-30, New York City.

AMERICAN ECONOMIC FOUNDATION (AEF)
51 East 42nd St.   Phone: (212) 687-5330
New York, N.Y. 10017
Fred G. Clark, Chm.
Founded 1939 - Supporters 18,000 - Staff 20. "Supporters are persons
interested in applied research of simplified vocabulary in the field
of economics at the mass level, including primary and secondary
classrooms." Seeks to locate the causes of, and find remedies for,
friction between economic groups. Maintains a library of 1000
volumes on economics and sociology. Publications: (1) Economics
Facts of Life, monthly; (2) The Fallacies We Live By, monthly; also
publishes occasional books, pamphlets, and booklets.

AMERICAN INSTITUTE FOR ECONOMIC RESEARCH (AIER)
Great Barrington, Mass. 01230   Phone: (413) 528-0140
C. Russell Doane, Dir.
Founded 1934 - Members 6000 - Staff 70. "To provide, by research
and publications, information on economic and financial subjects that
is dependable and completely independent of special interests." Has a
fellowship program for graduate study at the Institute. Since 1963,
financial and advisory services rendered for AIER by American Institute
Counselors. Divisions: Research on General Economic Problems
(e.g. money-credit studies, business cycles); Research on Personal
Economic Problems (Investment section, Insurance section). Publications: (1) Research Reports, weekly; (2) Investment Bulletin, semi-
monthly; (3) Economic Education Bulletins, monthly; also publishes
educational bulletins on personal and general economic problems.

ASSOCIATION FOR COMPARATIVE ECONOMIC STUDIES (ACES)
Department of Economics   Phone: (815) 753-1023
Northern Illinois University   (815) 753-1100
DeKalb, Ill. 60115
Jack W. Skeels, Sec.-Treas.
Founded 1972. Economists and other social scientists from universities,
government, and business. To study comparative economic systems
and economic planning and to examine the impact of political and
social actions as they impinge upon economic systems. Cooperates
with other professional societies in arranging meetings for presentation of papers within the scope of comparative economics and
economic planning. Publications: (1) Bulletin, 3/year; (2) Newsletter. Formed by merger of: Association for the Study of Soviet-
Type Economies (founded 1959) and Association for Comparative
Economics (founded 1963).

ASSOCIATION FOR EVOLUTIONARY ECONOMICS (AFEE)
120 Boucke Building
Pennsylvania State Univ.
University Park, Pa. 16802
John C. Spychalski, Sec.-Treas.
Founded 1963 - Member 900. Economists; includes social scientists
"who profess sociology, economic history, anthropology, etc." To
foster interest in the development of economics as an evolutionary
rather than static and/or mathematical science; to engage in economic
research and the diffusion of economic knowledge; to establish better
channels of communication among dissenting, non-Marxian economists.
Publication: Journal of Economic Issues, quarterly. Formerly: Ward-
man Group. Holds annual meeting, with American Economic Association.

ASSOCIATION FOR SOCIAL ECONOMICS
College of Saint Teresa   Phone: (501) 454-2930
Winona, Minn. 55987
Sister M. Yolande, Sec.-Treas.
Founded 1941 - Members 400 - Regional groups 12. Professional
society of economists, both business and academic. Promotes scientific
discussion of economic problems requiring a knowledge of both economic science and Christian social philosophy. Normative economics and
social policy are, therefore, the prime orientation of the organization.
Publications: (1) Review of Social Economy, semiannual; (2) Newsletter, semiannual. Formerly: Catholic Economic Association. Con-
vention/Meeting: Annual - held with American Economic Association.

ASSOCIATION FOR THE STUDY OF THE GRANTS ECONOMY (ASGE)
210 Prentis Bldg.   (Economic)
Wayne State University   Phone: (313) 577-4508
Detroit, Mich. 48202
Martin Pfaff, Sec.
Founded 1968 - Members 600. Social scientists who have been or are
currently, involved in teaching, research, or administration of programs
related to private or public transfers. "The objective of ASGE is to
foster the development of a theory of non-market economic phenomena,
as well as to study transfer components in the economy empirically,
and derive policy conclusions." Has cosponsored symposia on related
topics with the American Economic Association, the Association for
the Advancement of Science, and a number of other national associations. Independent research on the Grants Economy is carried out
by several members. Publication: Newsletter, 3-4/year; also
publishes Grants Economics Series (books). Holds annual symposium.

BUSINESS COUNCIL (Economic)
888 17th St., N.W.   Phone: (202) 298-7650
Washington, D.C. 20006
John W. Burke, Jr. Exec. Sec.
Founded 1933 - Members 200 - Staff 3. Business executives. "To
submit to any branch or agency of government a constructive point of
view on matters of public policy affecting the business interests of
the country; to respond to requests by the government for advice and
assistance in carrying out the responsibilities of any branch or agency;
to provide a medium for better understanding of government problems
by business." Most Council members are chairmen or presidents of
large corporations. Committee: Domestic Economy. Liaison committees: Council of Economic Advisers; Departments of Commerce;
Defense; Health, Education and Welfare; Housing and Urban Development; Labor; Treasury; Office of Management and Budget; The White
House. Publishes membership and committee list. Formerly: (1961)
Business Advisory Council. Meets quarterly.

COMMITTEE FOR ECONOMIC DEVELOPMENT (CED)
477 Madison Ave.   Phone: (212) 688-2063
New York, N.Y. 10022
Alfred C. Neal, Pres.
Founded 1942 - Trustees 200 - Staff 52. Not a membership organization. Nonpartisan group of businessmen and scholars who conduct
research and formulate policy recommendations on major economic
issues. Through its studies and reports seeks to contribute to full employment, higher living standards and increasing opportunities for all;
to promote economic growth and stability, and to strengthen the concepts and institutions essential to progress in a free society. Research
has included education; national economic policy; international economics; international trade and development; government management;
urban and area studies (area development, urban poverty, etc.); cor-
porate management. Conducts local and regional Policy Forums for
discussion, research and economic policy recommendations by local
businessmen and educators. Maintains private library of 5000 volumes.
Committee: Research and Policy, with sub-committees of Decision
Making for National Security; Economic and Social Impact of the New
Broadcast Media; Financing the Nation's Housing Needs; Improving
Productivity in Government; Improving the Quality of the Environment;
Management and Financing of Colleges; Organization and Financing of
a National Health Care System; Reform of the International Monetary
System; Reform of the Tax System; United States and Japan in a New
World Economy. Publications: (1) Newsletter; (2) Statements on
National Policy (subcommittee reports and recommendations); also
publishes books, booklets, and supplementary research papers.

Fig. 1. *Encyclopedia of Associations.* (Reproduced by permission of Gale Research
Association.)

BRITISH PSYCHOLOGICAL SOCIETY, 18-19 Albemarle Street, London, W1X 4DN. Founded 1901. This learned society is also a professional association. Its divisions and sections cover all aspects of psychology, and it holds conferences and meetings and conducts examinations. It has an information service available to all inquirers, and publishes five journals, including *British Journal of Psychology, British Journal of Social and Clinical Psychology, British Journal of Mathematical and Statistical Psychology,* and *British Journal of Educational Psychology.* There is also a Bulletin, an annual report, and a list of members.

BRITISH SOCIOLOGICAL ASSOCIATION, 13 Endsleigh Street, London, WC 1. Founded 1951. This society is concerned with promotion of interest in and advancement of the study and application of sociology in the United Kingdom. It has an information service available to all serious inquirers, has a section for sociology teachers, and holds conferences and meetings. Its journal is *Sociology.*

ECONOMIC HISTORY SOCIETY, Peterhouse, Cambridge. Founded 1927. This organization combines the functions of a learned society and a research body, and aims to encourage research into and the study of economic history. It has a section devoted to urban history, and holds an annual conference. Its journal is *Economic History Review.*

ECONOMIC RESEARCH COUNCIL, 10 Upper Berkeley Street, London, W 1. Founded 1943. The Council aims to promote education in the science of economics with particular reference to monetary policy, and acts as both a learned society and a research group. It holds meetings, provides education and training facilities, and has a collection of statistics as well as an information service. Its journal is *Economic Age,* and it publishes monographs and occasional papers.

ECONOMICS ASSOCIATION, 110 Banstead Road South, Sutton, Surrey. Founded 1946. This body caters primarily for teachers of economics and aims to promote the study of the subject in schools and colleges. Its journal is *Economics.* There is also a bulletin which is available only to members.

INSTITUTE OF COMMUNITY STUDIES, 18 Victoria Park Square, London, E 2. Founded 1954. This is a research organization concerned with all aspects of community life. Its reports are published through Routledge and Kegan Paul.

INSTITUTE OF ECONOMIC AFFAIRS LTD., 2 Lord North Street, London, W 1. Founded 1956. This group aims to promote the extension of public understanding of economic principles and their applications to practical problems. It holds meetings, and conferences, has an education and training programme and undertakes research. It collects statistics and has an information service available to all serious inquirers. As well as research reports, monographs, and occasional papers it publishes the *Hobart Papers,* which are intended for the general reader.

INSTITUTE OF RACE RELATIONS, 36 Jermyn Street, London, SW 1. Founded 1958. This research body sponsors research into relations between racial groups in Britain and gives advice on proposals for minimizing tensions. It collects statistics, holds conferences and meetings, has study groups, and an information service. It publishes *Race, Race Today,* monographs, bibliographies, a research register, and an annual report.

NATIONAL INSTITUTE OF ECONOMIC AND SOCIAL RESEARCH, 2 Dean Trench Street, London, SW 1. Founded 1938. This body carries out research and publishes the results in monographs through the Cambridge University Press. Its journal is the *National Institute Economic Review.*

NATIONAL INSTITUTE OF INDUSTRIAL PSYCHOLOGY, 14 Welbeck Street, London W1M 8DR. Founded 1921. The Institute combines the functions of a learned society, a research organization, and a professional association. It has an education and training programme, and it maintains a library and information service. Its journals are *Occupational Psychology* and *NIIP Bulletin,* and it issues an annual report.

POLITICAL AND ECONOMIC PLANNING, 12 Upper Belgrave Street, London, SW 1. Founded 1931. This group aims to contribute to more effective planning and policy making by government and industry by studying selected problems and publishing the results of their work in the form of *Planning Broadsheets,* reports, and monographs.

POLITICAL STUDIES ASSOCIATION OF THE UNITED KINGDOM, London School of Economics and Political Science, Houghton Street, Aldwych, London, WC 2. Founded 1950. This is both a learned society and a professional association which aims to further the development of political studies. It has study groups and holds an annual conference. Its journal is *Political Studies.*

REGIONAL STUDIES ASSOCIATION, 45 Notting Hill Gate, London, W 11. Founded 1965. This professional association holds meetings and conferences, and has an information service which is only available to its members. Its journal is *Regional Studies.*

ROYAL ANTHROPOLOGICAL INSTITUTE OF GREAT BRITAIN AND IRELAND, 21 Bedford Square, London, WC 1. Founded 1843. The RAI is both a learned society and an organization which carries out research. Its aims are to promote the study of the science of man. It has several specialist groups, including ethnographic films and cultural history. It holds conferences and meetings and has study groups. Its library has an international reputation and there is an information service available to all inquirers. Publications include: *Man: Journal of the RAI, Proceedings . . ., Index of Current Periodicals Received in the Library . . .*, and occasional papers.

ROYAL ECONOMIC SOCIETY, Marshall Library, Sidgwick Avenue, Cambridge, CB3 9DB. Founded 1903. This learned body holds meetings, publishes monographs, and the *Economic Journal.*

SCOTTISH ECONOMIC SOCIETY, C/o The Department of Political Economy, The University, St. Andrews. Founded 1954. The aims of this learned society are to study economic and social problems "in accordance with the Scottish tradition of political economy inspired by Adam Smith". To this end it holds regular meetings throughout Scotland. It publishes *Scottish Journal of Political Economy.*

SOCIETY OF BUSINESS ECONOMISTS, 16 Beechpark Way, Watford, Herts. Founded 1960. This society caters for the needs of practising economists in industry and commerce. It holds an annual conference and publishes *Business Economics* and *Proceedings* of the conferences.

TAVISTOCK INSTITUTE OF HUMAN RELATIONS, Tavistock Centre, Belsize Lane, London, NW 3. Founded 1947. The aim of this research body is to study human relations in conditions of wellbeing, conflict, or breakdown, in the family, the work group, and the larger organization. It also has functions of a professional association in that it has an education and training programme. Its library is one of the best in the field. Its journal is *Human Relations.*

United States

AMERICAN ACADEMY OF POLITICAL AND SOCIAL SCIENCES, 3937 Chestnut Street, Philadelphia, Pa 19104. Founded 1889. This is a learned society and research body which draws its members from qualified social scientists and publishes the papers read at its meetings in *Annals.* It has a limited information service, but inquirers are referred to appropriate member specialists.

AMERICAN ANTHROPOLOGICAL ASSOCIATION, 1703 New Hampshire Avenue NW, Washington, DC 20009. This is a professional association, which holds meetings and conferences throughout the United States. It publishes *American Anthropologist* and *Anthropological Studies.*

AMERICAN ECONOMIC ASSOCIATION, Rendigs Fels, 1313 21st Avenue South, Nashville, Tennessee, 37212. Founded 1885. This learned society cum professional association aims to foster and encourage the study and application of economics to present-day problems. It holds meetings and congresses throughout the United States, and it has an employment register. Its publications include *American Economic Review, Journal of Economic Literature, Proceedings,* and several monographs, some in association with the Royal Economic Society.

AMERICAN INSTITUTE FOR ECONOMIC RESEARCH, Great Barrington, Mass. 01230. Founded 1934. The Institute aims to carry out research and to publish the results. It provides information on economic subjects that is "dependable and totally independent of special interests", and has an undergraduate scholarship programme and a fellowship programme for graduate study in the Institute. It publishes weekly research reports, *Investment Bulletin,* and *Economic News.*

AMERICAN POLITICAL SCIENCE ASSOCIATION, 1527 New Hampshire Avenue NW, Washington, DC 20036. Founded 1903. Publishes *American Political Science Review,* and apart from holding meetings and conferences it has been active in studying the bibliographical needs of political scientists.

AMERICAN PSYCHOLOGICAL ASSOCIATION, 1200 17th Street NW, Washington, DC 20036. Founded 1892. This professional association also undertakes and sponsors research. It publishes thirteen journals and an employment bulletin.

AMERICAN SOCIETY FOR PUBLIC ADMINISTRATION, 1225 Connecticut Avenue NW, Washington, DC 20036. Founded 1939. The aims of this body are wide: it is concerned not only with the development of the study of the subject but also with carrying out research. It holds national and regional conferences, maintains an employment register, and publishes *Public Administration Review* and *Public Administration News and Views.*

AMERICAN SOCIOLOGICAL ASSOCIATION, 1722 North Street NW, Washington, DC 20036. Founded 1905. The Association seeks to stimulate and improve research, instruction, and discussion, and to encourage co-operation among sociologists. Its membership includes qualified sociologists, students, and interested laymen, and its range of journals caters for all levels of interest. It has an information and referral service, and holds meetings and conferences throughout the United States. Its journals are *American Sociological Review, Contemporary Sociology: a Journal of*

Reviews, The American Sociologist, Journal of Health and Social Behavior, and as well as publishing monographs it sponsors *Sociological Methodology* and *Issues and Trends in Sociology.*

AMERICAN SOCIOMETRIC ASSOCIATION, 259 Wolcott Avenue, Beacon, NY, USA. Founded 1946. This group caters for those interested in the applications of mathematics to sociology, sociometry, social psychology, psychology, and education. Its journal is *International Journal of Sociometry and Sociatry.*

ECONOMETRIC SOCIETY, Box 1264, Yale Station, New Haven, Connecticut, USA. Founded 1930. This body is specifically concerned with the advancement of economic theory in its relation to statistics and mathematics, and promoting the unification of the theoretical – quantitative and the empirical – quantitative approach to economic problems. Its journal is *Econometrica.*

SOUTHERN SOCIOLOGICAL SOCIETY, University of Georgia, Athens, Georgia 30601. Founded 1965. This is an example of the many societies which are affiliated to national bodies – in this case the American Sociological Association – and which publish their own journals. SSS issue *Southern Sociologist* and *Social Forces.*

INTERNATIONAL ORGANIZATIONS

As well as the national associations there are international organizations which exist to advance the study of their subjects throughout the world and encourage international co-operation of specialists. Most are concerned with the application of their subject to present-day problems, aim to encourage research and the dissemination of information, and hold international congresses and round-table discussions. Membership of most of these organizations consists of representatives from national associations, and most are affiliated to or were formed under the aegis of UNESCO. The organizations listed below are those which have made some contribution to the international development of their subject.

INTERNATIONAL SOCIAL SCIENCE COUNCIL, Unesco House, 1 rue Miollis 75 – Paris 15e, France. Founded 1952. The aims of this body are to advance social sciences throughout the world and to develop their applications to the major problems of the day; to develop co-operation between social scientists at an international level; to arrange for the interpretation and comparison of results of social science research; to ensure permanent contact between social science organizations; to encourage and co-ordinate internationally the diffusion of information regarding publications in the social sciences and related subjects; to advise the United Nations on any questions which may be referred to it; to propose to the appropriate international bodies specific research projects which are multi-disciplinary in character and international in interest. It holds meetings, seminars, round-table conferences, and general assemblies, and its membership consists of representatives from other international non-government organizations. It publishes *Social Science Information*, working papers, and reports and proceedings of its meetings. It has established social science centres in several countries where none existed, and training programmes for social scientists.

INTERNATIONAL COMMITTEE FOR SOCIAL SCIENCES DOCUMENTATION, Unesco House, 1 rue Miollis 75 – Paris 15ᵉ, France. Founded 1950. The main function of this body is to stimulate and co-ordinate various bibliographies and other publications of interest to social scientists, and it has stimulated the production of abstracting services by advising other international associations. It was responsible for the *International Bibliography of the Social Sciences, World List of Social Science Periodicals, International Register of Current Team Research in the Social Sciences,* and *World Index of Social Science Institutions.*

INTERNATIONAL ECONOMIC ASSOCIATION, 54 bd Raspail, 75 – Paris 6ᵉ, France. Founded 1950. It holds round-table conferences and discussions, and aims to encourage the provision of international media for the dissemination of economic thought and knowledge, and shares some of the responsibility for the *International Bibliography of Economics.* It publishes *International Economic Papers,* reports, and papers.

INTERNATIONAL ECONOMIC HISTORY ASSOCIATION, Eidgenössische Technische Hochschule Bureau G27.3, Leonhardstrasse 33, 8006, Zurich, Switzerland. Founded 1965. This society, which is not affiliated to UNESCO in any formal manner, aims to promote personal contact between historians in all countries; to organize scientific meetings, and to encourage all publications aiming at developing and spreading knowledge of economic history. It publishes the proceedings of its conferences.

INTERNATIONAL POLITICAL SCIENCE ASSOCIATION, 43 rue des Champs-Elysées, 1050 Brussels, Belgium. Founded 1949. This organization has the standard aims of the international associations which are linked to UNESCO, but its membership extends to individuals as well as national representatives. It is responsible for *International Political Science Abstracts* and *International Bibliography of Political Science,* and publishes monographs and reports of its meetings and conferences.

INTERNATIONAL SOCIOLOGICAL ASSOCIATION, Via Daverio 7, 20122, Milan, Italy. Founded 1949. This UNESCO-sponsored association has established eleven research committees on different aspects of sociology, such as sociology of law, of medicine, of popular culture and leisure, political sociology, psychiatric sociology, and urban and rural sociology. It holds triennial congresses and publishes *Current Sociology.* It is partly responsible with the American Sociological Association for the production of *Sociological Abstracts,* and has produced special bibliographies.

INTERNATIONAL UNION OF ANTHROPOLOGICAL AND ETHNO-LOGICAL SCIENCES, C/o The Department of Sociology and Anthropology, University of Waterloo, Ontario, Canada. Founded 1948. Like the other bodies which are affiliated to and form part of the UNESCO overall plan for international associations in the social sciences, this association holds meetings and congresses, and aims to contribute to the international development of the scientific study of its subject. Its membership consists of representatives from national associations, and it is partly responsible for the *International Bibliography of Social and Cultural Anthropology.*

INTERNATIONAL UNION FOR THE SCIENTIFIC STUDY OF POPULA-TION, 5 rue Forgeur, 4000 Liege, Belgium. Founded 1918. This organization aims to advance the progress of quantitative and qualitative demography by publications, holding congresses, and by encouraging personal contacts. It tries to stimulate interest in demography among national and international institutions and the general public. Its journal is *Le Démographe,* and it publishes monographs and conference reports.

WORLD ASSOCIATION FOR PUBLIC OPINION RESEARCH, C/o Roper Public Opinion Research Center, Box 624, Williamstown, Mass., 01267. Founded 1947. This organization aims to promote understanding among the peoples of the world through facilitating and encouraging "honest, accurate and useful surveying concerning their opinions, knowledge, behavior, needs, hopes, fears and ideals". It holds conferences, of which it publishes the proceedings, and it issues a *Newsletter.*

WORLD FEDERATION FOR MENTAL HEALTH, C/o The Department of Psychiatry, University of the West Indies, Mona, Kingston 7, Jamaica. Founded 1948. The Federation aims to promote among all peoples and all nations the highest possible standard of mental health in its broadest biological, medical, educational, and social aspects. It holds meetings and congresses and is the centre of the Clearing House for Information on Mental Health. It publishes *World Mental Health Bulletin,* proceedings of meetings and conferences, annual reports and monographs.

CHAPTER 4

Books

The volume of new books appearing annually in the social sciences is constantly increasing: in England during 1972, some five and a half thousand titles were published. How is the social scientist to keep abreast of this volume of material and to know what is likely to be of most use? How is he to be aware of the vast amount of older material, much of which is no longer in print, but which is still available in libraries? It is important that he makes the best possible use of the sources of information which are available, because if he does not he is likely to miss important material. He cannot rely on chance to find key works, and the hours spent in searching for the literature will be worth while, as it could save considerable time in re-writing at a later date.

REVIEWS

Specialist periodicals are useful as sources of information on new books because they frequently carry review sections, some of which are quite substantial. Book reviews vary considerably in length and usefulness, the long reviews not necessarily being the most helpful. A short review usually indicates the scope of the work and assesses its value, generally indicating the author's standpoint where this is relevant. Journals which have a policy of short reviews usually have a policy of covering large numbers of works, sometimes over sixty in one issue. Other journals have a policy of devoting several pages to one title, and giving a critical analysis which can sometimes obviate the need to read the book. This latter kind of review is clearly most useful where the work is likely to be of only marginal interest to the reader. The review should at all events reflect the contents of the work accurately enough to enable the reader to decide how relevant it will be to his area of interest.

No guide can be given as to the relative value of reviews in individual journals, but generally those which devote greatest space to book reviews will be more likely to cover most of the new literature. However, despite the fact that most journals have review sections, at least 30 per cent of all social science material never gets reviewed, and the currency of many reviews is poor, partly because many of the journals which carry reviews are issued only quarterly, or even less frequently. It is only the general review journals, such as *The Times Literary Supplement* (London, Times Newspapers, issued weekly) and *The New York Times Book Review* (The New York Times Co., New York, issued weekly), which can hope to be current, but as they are reviewing books on all subjects, they can only cover a small part of the output of any one area.

Reviews are particularly useful for foreign-language publications, since the books they describe might take a long time to translate, and the average researcher may find them difficult to obtain if he is unfamiliar with the bibliographical services provided by foreign countries or because the books are not on general sale in this country. There are very few book shops which hold large stocks of foreign-language publications.

Most of the journals listed in Chapter 5 include book reviews, but the following are particularly useful in their subject areas:

British Journal of Sociology (London, Routledge & Kegan Paul, for the London School of Economics, 1950- , issued quarterly). This journal usually has two long and highly critical reviews in each issue, plus several short ones. The bias is towards British publications, but representative material from elsewhere is reviewed.

Contemporary Sociology (Washington, American Sociological Association, 1972- , issued bi-monthly). This journal is devoted entirely to reviewing new books, and is reasonably current, reviewing most books within six months of their appearance. Coverage of English-language publications is wide, but is weaker for books in foreign languages.

Economic Journal (London, Royal Economic Society, 1891- , issued quarterly). There are about thirty long reviews in each issue, covering all aspects of economics, and with foreign items very well represented.

Journal of Economic Literature (Evanston, Ill., American Economic Association, 1969- , issued quarterly). Rather than a traditional journal carrying articles on a variety of subjects, this publication is a collection of abstracts and reviews, with some 300 books being reviewed annually.

Political Studies (London, Oxford University Press, for the Political Studies Association, 1953- , issued quarterly). There are extensive book reviews in this publication, with some British bias, but books from other countries are well represented.

Political Science Quarterly (New York, Academy of Political Science, 1886-). Reviews books on historical and contemporary political, economic, and social questions, with a pronounced American bias.

Anyone wishing to know where reviews of specific books have appeared should consult *Book Review Digest* (New York, H. W. Wilson, 1905- , issued monthly) which is an index of reviews of English-language books appearing in seventy-three British and American journals. It is arranged alphabetically by the author of the book being reviewed, and in order to be listed the book must have had at least two reviews. With the same purpose, but wider in coverage, is *Book Review Index* (Detroit, Gale Research, 1965- , issued monthly) which indexes reviews in 215 general, specialized, and scholarly publications. Like *BRD*, it is arranged alphabetically by the author of the book. *Index to Book Reviews in the Humanities* (Detroit, Philip Thomson, issued annually) is similar, extending the term "humanities" to include social sciences, and indexes reviews in 700 periodicals, mostly in English.

A useful guide to the same kinds of information from other countries and in other languages is Richard A. Gray's *A Guide to Book Review Citations: a bibliography of sources* (Ohio State University Press, 1968), which lists not only all indexes to reviews, but also all journals, in classified order, which regularly carry book reviews.

ADVERTISEMENTS

Periodicals contribute to the supply of information about new books in two other ways: through the advertisements they carry, and through the lists of newly printed and reprinted materials which most journals publish under the heading *Books Received* in each issue. Advertisements, being designed to enhance sales usually include details about the scope and intellectual level of the work they are publicizing. Their main value for the social scientist is that they can provide a starting point for his information search, as they often quote from reviews, albeit almost always favourably.

Most periodicals include a section listing new books. These, however, do not generally assess the value of the publications, although one journal which gives helpful brief annotations for each item is the *International Social Science Journal* (New York, UNESCO, 1949- , issued quarterly), which lists a total of some 300 books each year, with a good international coverage. In most other cases the only indication of the potential use of a work is to be found in its description. Titles are frequently vague in the social sciences;

often they are misleading, especially when works describe themselves as introductory when in fact a considerable amount of basic subject knowledge is required before they can be understood, and no gloassaries or definitions are given. Neither is the title any guide to the reliability or authority of the information a book contains. When the author is well known in a particular field there are no problems of assessment, and in any case his works will usually be reviewed. In the case of a first work there can be no such prejudgement, and there is less chance of the book being the subject of reviews.

Advertisement details from publishers who specialize in social sciences are helpful as a means of keeping aware of new books, and most publishers will send their catalogues, or details of new items, on request. Those who specialize in the social sciences include:

Great Britain

ALLEN & UNWIN LTD., Park Lane, Hemel Hempstead, Hertfordshire.

COLLIER-MACMILLAN LTD., Blue Star House, Highgate Hill, London, N 19.

HEINEMANN EDUCATIONAL BOOKS LTD., 48 Charles Street, London, W1X 8AH.

MACMILLAN PRESS LTD., Little Essex Street, London, WC2R 3LF.

METHUEN & CO. LTD., 11 New Fetter Lane, London, EC4P 4EE.

OXFORD UNIVERSITY PRESS, Ely House, 37 Dover Street, London, W1X 4AH.

ROUTLEDGE & KEGAN PAUL LTD., 68-74 Carter Lane, London, EC4.

TAVISTOCK PUBLICATIONS LTD., 11 New Fetter Lane, London, EC4P 4EE.

WEIDENFELD & NICOLSON LTD., 5 Winsley Street, Oxford Circus, London W1N 7AQ..

United States

ACADEMIC PRESS INC., 111 Fifth Avenue, New York, NY, 10003.

APPLETON-CENTURY-CROFTS INC., 440 Park Avenue South, New York, NY, 10016.

CROWELL, COLLIER & MACMILLAN INC., Macmillan Company, 886 Third Avenue, New York, NY, 10022.

HARPER & ROW PUBLISHERS INC., 49 East 33rd Street, New York, NY, 10016.

HUMANITIES PRESS INC., 303 Park Avenue South, New York, NY, 10010.

MCGRAW-HILL BOOK CO., 330 West 42nd Street, New York, NY, 10017.

OXFORD UNIVERSITY PRESS INC., 200 Madison Avenue, New York, NY, 10016.
|FREDERICK A. PRAEGER INC., 111 Fourth Avenue, New York, NY, 10003.
RANDOM HOUSE INC., 457 Madison Avenue, New York, NY, 10022.
SCARECROW PRESS INC., 52 Liberty Street, Box 656, Metuchen, NJ, 08840.

Several publishers also produce series of books in specific social science areas. These include: *International Library of Sociology and Social Reconstruction* issued by Routledge & Kegan Paul under the editorship of W. J. H. Sprott, covering all aspects of sociology. This series closed in 1973 with a total of almost 300 titles, and was replaced by three series, *International Library of Sociology; International Library of Social Policy;* and *International Library of Anthropology.* The same publishers issue the *Students' Library of Sociology,* which is edited by Roy Emerson, as a series of monographs, each providing a thorough introduction to a selected topic, at a deeper level than would be possible in a multi-topic introductory textbook.

There have recently been several new series in sociology, such as *Studies in Sociology*, edited by Anthony Giddens and published by Macmillan Press. This series is issued under the auspices of the British Sociological Association and is designed to provide short but comprehensive and scholarly treatment of key problem areas in the subject. *Aspects of Modern Sociology,* edited by John Barron Mays and Maurice Craft, issued by Longmans (Longman House, Burnt Mill, Harlow, Essex), is designed to offer an analysis of contemporary society through the study of basic demographic, ideological, and structural features, and through the study of such major social institutions as the family, education, economic, and political structure. Fontana Books (William Collins, Sons & Co. Ltd., 14 St. James's Place, London, SW 1) issue two series of paperbacks in sociology: Fontana, *Introduction to Sociology,* edited by Michael Banton and Theo Nichols, and *Readings in Sociology,* edited by Eric Butterworth and David Weir, which contains extracts of writings by key British and foreign sociologists together with short introductions to each area. Other series in sociology include: *The Making of Sociology,* edited by Ronald Fletcher (Thomas Nelson & Sons Ltd., 36 Park Lane, London, W1Y 4DE); and *Themes and Issues in Modern Sociology*, edited by Jean Floud and John H. Goldthorpe (Collier-Macmillan).

In economics, Prentice-Hall (70 Fifth Avenue, New York, NY, 10011) issue *Foundations of Modern Economics Series,* edited by Otto Eckstein; Heinemann issue *Studies in the British Economy,* edited by Derek Lee. The

Macmillan Studies in Economics, edited by D. C. Rowan and R. Fisher, aims to provide a critical survey of developments in theoretical and applied economics, and the same publishers also issue *Studies in Economic History,* edited by M. W. Flinn.

Studies in Comparative Politics is also issued by Macmillan, edited by S. E. Finer and Ghita Ionescu; this is a series of short monographs concerning changing theoretical approaches and methodological reappraisals. *Key Concepts in Political Science,* edited by Leonard Schapiro, is issued jointly by Macmillan (paperbacks) and Pall Mall Press Ltd. (5 Cromwell Place, London, SW 7); the latter issues the cloth-bound editions. These are short texts of the survey-and-introduction type. Nelson's *Basic Concepts in Political Science Series,* which is to be published in 1975, is to be a closed, integrated series which will consist of a core text and seven shorter volumes, and is intended to introduce first- and second-year university students to the study of politics and to the concepts now in use in the field. Fontana Books issue *Fontana Studies in Politics* and *World Economic Issues,* and their Modern Masters series will also be of interest to students of political science, as it includes such people as Lenin and Gandhi.

Most publishers take part in an information scheme which is used mainly by academics, whereby details of new publications in particular fields of user interest are sent to individuals. In Great Britain, Publishers Information Card Service (PICS), 8 Rathbone Place, London, W 1, supply details on cards, rather like catalogue cards, which contain not only bibliographical details of the books concerned, but also lists of contents, authors' qualifications, and intended readership. The International Book Information Service, New Building, North Circular Road, Neasden, London, NW 10, mail publishers' catalogues and information sheets, as well as some cards of the same kind as those mentioned above. The same body also operates in the United States, from 1 Park Avenue, New York, NY, 10016, and both services cover both British and American publications.

BIBLIOGRAPHIES

General Current

Those wishing to see books as soon as possible after their publication should consult current bibliographies, which are designed to list books as soon as possible after their publication. Because it is expensive to produce current bibliographies in limited subject areas, these tend not to be as frequent as general bibliographies which are usually of a country's total publishing output. Therefore it is important for the researcher who wishes to be really up to date to consult the more general services. Many such services are classified, and therefore it is easy to find information on specific topics; those which have only an alphabetical approach by author, or keywords from titles, are clearly less useful for the subject approach.

The *British National Bibliography* (London, Council of the BNB Ltd., 1950- , issued weekly) (Fig. 2) lists all books, pamphlets, and a large number of government publications which are issued in the United Kingdom, and is based on the material deposited at the British Library (BL). Its currency is generally good, with the majority of items being recorded within a month of their publication, but unfortunately some publishers do not send their material to the BL until some months after their issue, and this results in a delay between the book being available and its being recorded in the bibliography. The *BNB* is arranged according to the Dewey Decimal Classification scheme, and each class mark is given an adjacent subject heading, this making subject searching easier, as the subject of any item can be seen at a glance regardless of how descriptive or otherwise its title. As many American publishers, such as Addison-Wesley, McGraw-Hill, and Wiley, have British offices, their publications are also listed in this bibliography, thus giving it further value. The main disadvantage of the work is that no annotations are given to show the level of each item; the information in each entry is limited to bibliographical description, and therefore it is not always easy to assess the possible value of each publication listed. Regular cumulations of up to five years make the work useful for retrospective searching.

If even greater currency than the *BNB* is required, it is possible to use *The Bookseller* (London, Whitaker, 1858- , issued weekly), which is a trade list of commercially issued books. It is an alphabetical author and title list, and therefore only of value in a subject search if the title of relevant works contains suitable keywords. *The Bookseller* has monthly cumulations, and a quarterly bibliography based on the entries it records is *Cumulative Book List* (London, Whitaker, 1924-), which, as well as an author and title list, contains a broadly classified section to allow for a subject approach. There are annual cumulations.

For books issued in the United States the *American Book Publishing Record* (Bowker, New York, 1960- , issued monthly) performs much the same function as does the *BNB*. It is arranged by the DC scheme, and is more useful than its British counterpart in that many of the items are given brief annotations which indicate scope and for whom the work is intended. Unlike the *BNB*, the *American Book Publishing Record* is a commercial publication

325.3 — COLONISATION
325'.342'09624 — Sudan. Colonial administration by Great Britain,
        1922-1953. *Personal observations*
Robertson, *Sir* James
    Transition in Africa: from direct rule to independence: a memoir/
    by Sir James Robertson; with a foreword by Margery Perham. —
    London: C. Hurst, 1974. — xiv,272p,[8]p of plates: ill, 2 maps,
    ports; 25cm.
    Index.
    ISBN 0 903983 06 0 : £4.80
    Also classified at 325'.342'09669
    1.Ti
                                                              (B74-04505)

325'.342'09669 — Nigeria. Colonial administration by Great Britain,
        1955-1960. *Personal observations*
Robertson, *Sir* James
    Transition in Africa: from direct rule to independence: a memoir/
    by Sir James Robertson; with a foreword by Margery Perham. —
    London: C. Hurst, 1974. — xiv,272p,[8]p of plates: ill, 2 maps,
    ports; 25cm.
    Index.
    ISBN 0 903983 06 0 : £4.80
    Primary classification 325'.342'09624
    1.Ti

325.4/9 — INTERNATIONAL MIGRATION BY LOCALITY
325.6 — Africa. Colonial administration, 1870-1960
Gann, Lewis Henry
    Colonialism in Africa, 1870-1960/ edited by L.H. Gann and Peter
    Duignan. — London: Cambridge University Press.
    In 5 vols.
    Vol.5: A bibliographical guide to colonialism in sub-Sahara Africa/ by Peter
    Duignan and L.H. Gann. — 1973. — xii,552p; 24cm.
    Index.
    ISBN 0 521 07859 8 : £9.00
    1.Ti 2.Duignan, Peter
                                                              (B74-04506)

327 — FOREIGN RELATIONS
327'.09171'3 — Western bloc countries. Foreign relations with
        communist countries, 1917-1960
Higgins, Hugh
    The Cold War/ [by] Hugh Higgins. — London: Heinemann
    Educational, 1974. — ix,141p: ill, facsims, maps, ports; 22cm. —
    (Studies in modern history)
    Bibl.: p.134-138. — Index.
    ISBN 0 435 31395 9 : £2.50
    ISBN 0 435 31397 5 Pbk: £1.00
    Also classified at 327'.09171'7
    1.Ti 2.Sr
                                                              (B74-04507)

327'.09171'7 — Communist countries. Foreign relations with Western
        bloc countries, 1917-1960
Higgins, Hugh
    The Cold War/ [by] Hugh Higgins. — London: Heinemann
    Educational, 1974. — ix,141p: ill, facsims, maps, ports; 22cm. —
    (Studies in modern history)
    Bibl.: p.134-138. — Index.
    ISBN 0 435 31395 9 : £2.50
    ISBN 0 435 31397 5 Pbk: £1.00
    Primary classification 327'.09171'3
    1.Ti 2.Sr

327.3/9 — FOREIGN POLICIES OF SPECIAL COUNTRIES
327.47'073 — Russia. Foreign relations with United States, 1945-1972
Adomeit, Hannes
    Soviet risk-taking and crisis behaviour: from confrontation to
    coexistence?/ by Hannes Adomeit. — London: International
    Institute for Strategic Studies, 1973. — [3],40p; 25cm. — (Adelphi
    papers; no.101)
    ISBN 0 900492 66 x Sd: £0.35
    Also classified at 327.73'047
    1.Ti 2.Sr
                                                              (B74-04508)

328.42'005 — Great Britain. Parliament. *Yearboo*
    Dod's parliamentary companion. — Epsom: Sell
    1974: 142nd year: 161st issue. — [1974]. — ix,830p;
    Index.
    ISBN 0 85499 621 4 : £5.00

330 — ECONOMICS

Carter, Charles Frederick
    The science of wealth: an elementary textbook
    C.F. Carter. — 3rd ed. — London: Edward A
    213p: ill; 23cm.
    Previous ed.: 1967. — Index.
    ISBN 0 7131 5711 9 : £2.70
    ISBN 0 7131 5712 7 Pbk: £1.35
    1.Ti

330'.01'84 — Econometric models. Applications of
        theory
Weintraub, E Roy
    General equilibrium theory/ [by] E. Roy Weir
    Macmillan, 1974. — 64p: ill; 21cm. — (Macm
    economics)
    ISBN 0 333 14460 0 Pbk: £0.75
    1.Ti

330.9 — ECONOMIC CONDITIONS
330.9'37'06 — Ancient Rome. Economic conditions
Duncan-Jones, Richard
    The economy of the Roman Empire: quantitat
    Richard Duncan-Jones. — London: Cambridg
    1974. — xvi,396p; 24cm.
    Bibl.: p.370-378. — Index.
    ISBN 0 521 20165 9 : £7.60
    1.Ti

330.9'42'085 — Great Britain. Economic policies
Lee, Derek
    Control of the economy/ by Derek Lee; edited
    Anthony. — London: Heinemann Educational
    ill; 20cm. — (Studies in the British economy)
    Bibl.: p.129-131. — Index.
    ISBN 0 435 84542 x Pbk: £0.60
    1:Ti 2.Anthony, Vivian Stanley 3.Sr

330.9'51'05 — China. Economic conditions, 1952-1
Swamy, Subramanian
    Economic growth in China and India, 1952-19
    appraisal/ [by] Subramanian Swamy. — Chica
    University of Chicago Press, 1973. — ix,85p; 2
    This work also appeared as volume 21, number 4, pa
    "Economic Development and Cultural Change", edite
    and published by the University of Chicago Press' - ti
    ISBN 0 226 78315 4 : £3.15
    Also classified at 330.9'54'04
    1.Ti

330.9'54'04 — India (Republic). Economic conditi
Swamy, Subramanian
    Economic growth in China and India, 1952-19
    appraisal/ [by] Subramanian Swamy. — Chica
    University of Chicago Press, 1973. — ix,85p; 2
    This work also appeared as volume 21, number 4, pa
    "Economic Development and Cultural Change", edite
    and published by the University of Chicago Press' - ti
    ISBN 0 226 78315 4 : £3.15
    Primary classification 330.9'51'05
    1.Ti

Fig. 2. *British National Bibliography.* (Reproduced by permission of the Council of
    the BNB Ltd.)

based on items recorded in the *Publishers' Weekly* (New York, Bowker, 1872-), and it therefore omits federal and state documents. The *Cumulative Book Index* (New York, Wilson, 1898- , issued monthly) has a somewhat wider scope than *American Book Publishing Record* as it claims to be a world list of books in the English language, and indeed items issued in countries other than the United States are well represented, although by no means exhaustively covered, but the currency of their inclusion leaves much to be desired. This bibliography has a dictionary catalogue arrangement, interfiling authors, titles, and subjects. The subject headings used are less precise than in those bibliographies which use a special classification scheme, but adequate references are provided between related headings, although it is undoubtedly more time consuming to use this work for a specific topic than to use those which allow for a more detailed arrangement. Like the other bibliographies, *Cumulative Book Index* has regular cumulations, the largest currently being for two years.

National bibliographies of other countries are also valuable for anyone making an exhaustive literature search. Apart from those listed below, details of those of other countries can be found in *Bibliographical Services Throughout the World, 1964-1969*, by P. Avicenne (Paris, UNESCO, 1972), which lists the major bibliographies of over 100 countries, and in A. J. Walford's *Guide to Reference Material* (London, The Library Association, 2nd edn., 1966-70, 3 vols.), of which a new edition is in preparation and due for completion in 1976.

Biblio: catalogue des ouvrages parus en langue française dans le monde entier (Paris, Hachette, 1933- , 10 issues a year) is the most easily used bibliography of French-language books, with very good international coverage, but is limited in scope to commercially published books. Each monthly issue contains bio-bibliographical sketches, which are not included in the annual cumulation, as well as some book reviews. It has a dictionary catalogue arrangement with good cross-references.

Bibliographie de la France (Paris, Cercle de la Libraire, 1811- , issued weekly) records material lodged at the Bibliothèque Nationale through legal deposit, and lists books, pamphlets, official publications, and special forms of material such as prints. Each issue has three main parts: *Bibliographie Officielle*, which is a classified list of books, pamphlets, and other materials, with supplements from time to time on theses, government publications, periodicals, atlases, music, etc.; *Chroniques*, which is basically concerned with publishing news; *Annonces*, which contains advertising material and a classified list: *Les Livres de la Semaine*, which cumulates monthly, quarterly, and annually, as *Les Livres de l'Année;* this cumulation also including items which appeared in *Bibliographie Officielle* but not in *Announces.*

Deutsche Nationalbibliographie (Leipzig, Verlag Für Buch-und Bibliothekswesen, monthly) is a bibliography in two parts. Part A lists commercially issued books from all German-speaking countries, and is classified in twenty-four sections. Part B is issued only semi-monthly, arranged in the same way as Part A, and is for books outside the book trade, dissertations, government publications, reports, etc. There are author and keyword indexes for each issue, and these cumulate quarterly. It is an official bibliography, based on material deposited at the Deutsche Bucherei. *Deutsche Bibliographie* (Frankfurt am Main, Buchhändler-Vereinigung GmbH, 1947- , issued weekly) is the West German counterpart of the Leipzig bibliography, and in many respects duplicates the material in that work. Both works have annual and quinquennial cumulations, but the West German work omits periodicals and dissertations.

General: Retrospective

Because the social scientist needs to use older material more frequently than does the pure scientist or technologist, it is essential that he is aware of the many tools which can enable him to exploit this material with the minimum of difficulty. The catalogues of national libraries, where these have classified arrangements, are, of course, excellent as retrospective bibliographies. Unfortunately for these purposes, most national libraries in the past saw as their main function the conservation rather than exploitation of material, and because of this many compiled only author catalogues. *The British Museum Subject Index of Modern Works Acquired Since 1881* (London, Trustees of the BM) is an alphabetical subject list of books in the BL, but excludes people as subjects, biographical and critical works being listed in the *General Catalogue of Printed Books.* . . . For those wanting information about books issued prior to 1881, R. A. Peddie's *Subject Index of Books Printed before 1880 and now in the British Museum* (London, Grafton, 1933-48, 4 vols.) is useful. Another useful source of information on older material on all subjects is the *Subject Index of the London Library* (London Library, 1909-55, 4 vols.), which is the subject catalogue of Britain's largest subscription library, and is strong in social science books.

For the United States the *Library of Congress Catalog. Books: Subjects* (Chicago, Mansell, 1945- , issued quarterly, with quinquennial cumulations) is the only subject guide to the Library of Congress's stock, but several university and public libraries have issued subject catalogues of their stocks from time to time, and these are useful sources of information, as, for example, the *Peabody Institute Catalog* (Baltimore, The Institute, 1883-1905, 13 vols.), which is a dictionary catalogue not only of books but also of parts of books, making it a useful index.

Bibliographies of Bibliographies

Individual subject bibliographies can be traced in bibliographies of bibliographies. Theodore Besterman's *A World Bibliography of Bibliographies* (Lausanne, Societas Bibliographica, 4th edn., 1965) is an extremely comprehensive list of separately published bibliographies from all over the world. It is arranged alphabetically by broad subject groups. *Index Bibliographicus* (The Hague, Federation Internationale de Documentation, 4th edn., 1959-64) in its second volume, *Social Sciences*, lists some 400 bibliographies. It is by no means comprehensive, but is valuable for locating older material, and because it is arranged by the Universal Decimal Classification scheme, is easy to use. *Bibliographic Index* (New York, Wilson, 1937- , issued semi-annually) is valuable because it lists not only separately published bibliographies but also those which appear as part of books or appended to journal articles. It is arranged alphabetically by subject and, apart from the obvious advantage of currency, it can be used as a retrospective tool since it has annual and quadrennial cumulations.

A major guide to bibliographies, and to other kinds of material such as dictionaries, periodicals, and other kinds of reference material, is *Les Sources du Travail Bibliographique* by Louise-Noëlle Malclès (Geneva, E. Droz, 1950-8, 4 vols.). The first volume of this work is concerned with general bibliographical services and bibliographies of bibliographies, and the second and third volumes cover the social sciences, listing special bibliographical services. Its international coverage is excellent, and it is not an over-statement to say that the work is the greatest contribution yet to bibliography. Another useful work is *Serial Bibliographies in the Humanities and Social Sciences* by Richard A. Gray (Ann Arbor, Mich., Pierian Press, 1969), which covers bibliographies, indexes, and abstracts.

Social Sciences

There are some useful guides to the literature of the social sciences as a whole which describe the organization of the social sciences and give details of significant publications in the field. The major work is *Sources of Information in the Social Sciences*, edited by C. M. White (New York, American Library Association, 2nd edn., 1973), which gives an outline of each major social science area together with important works in each field. Each section is then followed by a list of the major publications within various categories of material, such as periodicals, yearbooks, bibliographies, directories, etc. *A Reader's Guide to the Social Sciences,* edited by B. F. Hoselitz (New York, Free Press, 2nd edn., 1970), covers the textbook literature of eight social science areas, and is useful for those who wish to know the best material in any field. *The Literature of the Social Sciences* by Peter R. Lewis (London, The Library Association, 1960) is an introductory survey and guide to the major areas, and is particularly useful for its coverage of older materials which many of the other guides omit.

There are several bibliographies which limit themselves to the social sciences, though few are really current, for there is generally a considerable time-lag between the publication of a book and its appearance in a social science bibliography. A major contribution to current bibliography of the field is a series of four works sponsored by UNESCO: *International Bibliography of the Social Sciences* (London, Tavistock; New York, Aldine, 1952- , issued annually). The material is compiled by the International Committee for Social Science Documentation, and in total some 30,000 items are recorded each year. These entries are for books, periodical articles, and significant government publications, and there are brief annotations for many items. The bibliography is arranged according to a specially devised classification scheme, and has fairly detailed indexes, although there is room for improvement in these. The main problem with the bibliography is that although it is designed as a current service, there is a time-lag of up to two years before publication. As there have been no cumulations of this work, it is cumbersome to use for retrospective searching.

Another significant publication which covers virtually the whole of the social sciences is the *Bulletin of the Public Affairs Information Service* (New York, PAIS, 1915- , issued weekly), which is known generally as *PAIS*. This is a selective list of books, pamphlets, periodical articles, government publications, and reports relating to social and economic conditions, public administration, and international relations. Its scope is limited to English-language publications, theoretically from all over the world, but in fact with a distinct American bias. There are five cumulations throughout the year plus annual cumulations, and the work has some 30,000 entries each year. It is arranged alphabetically by subject, and its real value lies in its currency, with which no other service in the field can compete. It is complemented by *Foreign Language Index* (New York, PAIS, 1973- , issued quarterly), which extends the main service's coverage to the major West European languages.

SOCIAL SCIENCES - Bibliography (Cont'd.)

RAND CORPORATION. Social Science Department. A
selected list of unclassified publications of
the Social science Department, the Rand
Corporation, 1948-1962. Santa Monica, the
Corporation, 1962. pp. vii, 43. 28cm. (Rand
Corporation. Research Memoranda. 1403-9)

PARIS. Bibliothèque Nationale. Ouvrages
cyrilliques concernant les sciences sociales
et humaines: liste des reproductions dis-
ponibles; Cyrillic publications concerning
the social sciences and humanities. Paris,
Mouton, 1964-65. 2 vols.(in 1). 27cm.
(Paris. Ecole Pratique des Hautes Etudes.
Section des Sciences Economiques et Sociales.
Cahiers du Monde Russe et Soviétique.
Supplements, 1 and 2)

GRAHAM (IAN CHARLES CARGILL) and LIEB (BONNIE S.)
compilers. Publications of the Social Science
Department, the Rand Corporation, 1948-1964.
Santa Monica, the Corporation, 1964. pp. v,(74).
bibliog. 28cm. (Rand Corporation. Research
Memoranda. 3600)

LONDON. University. University College. Centre for
Urban Studies. Land use planning and the social
sciences: a selected bibliography: literature on
town and country planning and related social
studies in Great Britain, 1930-1963. London, the
Centre, 1964. pp. (v), 44. 24cm.

WHITE (CARL MILTON) and others, compilers.
Sources of information in the social
sciences: a guide to the literature.
Totowa, N.J., Bedminster Press, [1964].
pp. xiii, 498. 23½cm.

AMERICAN BEHAVIORAL SCIENTIST, THE. The A.B.S.
guide to recent publications in the social and
behavioral sciences. New York, the American
Behavioral Scientist, 1965. pp. xxi, 781.
23½cm.

BOEHM (ERIC H.) Blueprint for bibliography: a
system for the social sciences and humanities.
Santa Barbara, Calif., Clio Press, 1965.
pp. 34, 22. 28cm. (American Bibliographical
Center. Bibliography and Reference Series. No.1)

SPAIN. 1966. Catálogo de la biblioteca ([del]
Instituto Nacional de Estadística): obras
científicas; referido al 31 de diciembre de 1965
y suplemento de autores al 31 de diciembre de
1966, etc. (Instituto Nacional de Estadística)
Madrid, 1966. pp. 616. 21cm.

- Congresses

CONGRESO AMERICANO DE CIENCIAS SOCIALES, TUCUMAN,
1916. Memoria, etc. Buenos Aires, [imprint]
1917. pp. 971. 27cm.

CONFERENCE ON THE SOCIAL SCIENCES: THEIR RELATIONS
IN THEORY AND IN TEACHING, LONDON, 1935.
[Papers]. London, 1935. pp. (134). 21cm.

CONGRESSO NAZIONALE DI SCIENZE SOCIALI.
1. Congresso, 1958. L'integrazione
delle scienze sociali: città e campagna;
atti del primo Congresso, etc. Bologna,
Società Editrice il Mulino, [1958-9].
2 vols. bibliogs. 22cm.

Dictionaries and encyclopaedias

SUAVET (THOMAS) ed, Dictionnaire économique et
social. Paris, Editions Ouvrières, [1962]. pp.
455. bibliogs. 19cm. (Economie et Humanisme.
Initiation Economique. 3)

GOULD (JULIUS) and KOLB (WILLIAM L.) eds.
A dictionary of the social sciences; compiled
under the auspices of the United Nations
Educational, Scientific and Cultural Organization.
London, Tavistock Publications, 1964. pp. xvi, 76.
24½cm.

SUAVET (THOMAS) Dictionnaire économique et social.
3rd ed. Paris, Editions Ouvrières, [1965]. pp.
479. 18cm. (Economie et Humanisme. Initiation
Economique. 3)

OSNOVNYE... Основные понятия по об-
ществоведению: краткий словарь.
Москва, Политиздат, 1956. pp. 492.
13½cm.

INTERNATIONAL encyclopedia of the social
sciences; David L. Sills, editor.
[New York], Macmillan. [1968]. 17 vols.
bibliogs. 27½cm.

- History

SALOMON (ALBERT) In praise of enlightenment:
(essays in the history of ideas). Cleveland,
World Publishing Company, 1963. pp. 413.
20½cm. (Meridian Books. M 137)

- History - America, Latin

DAVIS (HAROLD EUGENE) ed. Latin American social
thought: the history of its development since
independence, with selected readings.
Washington, University Press of Washington,
[1963]. pp. ix, 558. bibliog. 21½cm.

- History - America, North

BOTTOMORE (THOMAS BURTON) Social criticism
in North America: (eight talks for CBC Radio
Toronto, Canadian Broadcasting Corporation,
[1966]. pp. v, 79. 20cm.

BOTTOMORE (THOMAS BURTON) Critics of
society: radical thought in North America:
[an expanded version of his Social
criticism in North America].
London, Allen and Unwin, 1967. pp. 143.
bibliog. 19½cm.

- History - Chile

JOBET (JULIO CÉSAR) Los precursores del pensamiento
social de Chile. Santiago de Chile, Editorial
Universitaria, 1955. 2 vols. (in 1). 14½cm.
(Colección Saber. 2,6)

Fig. 3. *A London Bibliography of the Social Sciences.* (Reproduced by permission of the
British Library of Political and Economic Science.)

Probably the most valuable retrospective tool for any social scientist is *A London Bibliography of the Social Sciences* (London School of Economics and Political Science/Mansell Information, 1931-) (Fig. 3), which is the catalogue of the BL of Political and Economic Science, with additional entries for the early period including other libraries of London University and the Royal Statistical Society, although it is now limited to the holding of the BLPES and the Edward Fry Library of International Law. This work is arranged alphabetically by subject, with variations in the headings used over the years, which, despite the copious cross-references, makes the work rather more time consuming to use than is ideal. Under each subject heading there are detailed subdivisions, including a section for government publications, which, whilst adding to the time it can take to use the work, results in a high degree of specificity, which is usually desirable. The *London Bibliography* ... is updated by a *Monthly List of Accessions,* arranged according to twenty-two broad subjects, within which works are listed chronologically. As so much of the material that this library buys or acquires is old, and in many cases no longer in print, it is useful to have a subsidiary arrangement by date of publication. From 1973 the main bibliography is to have annual computer-produced supplements, which will give it a currency to compare more than favourably with the *International Bibliography of the Social Sciences,* although it will not cover exactly the same ground, being limited to books and including fewer foreign-language items.

A highly selective service is the *ABS Guide to Recent Publications in the Social and Behavioral Sciences* (Beverly Hills, Sage, 1965), which was based on the entries that appeared in the *New Studies* section of the *American Behavioral Scientist* from 1957 to 1964. The main volume is classified and has some 6500 annotated entries covering books, pamphlets, government publications, and periodical articles, and it differs from the *PAIS* in that many of the entries are for foreign-language items. It is updated by an annual supplement, which is in turn kept up to date by the entries in the journal. Although it is highly selective and covers only a very small proportion of the output in the field, unlike the *London Bibliography* ... it can usefully supplement this latter work because of the helpful annotations.

Another publication from the same source as *ABS* is the *Universal Reference System* (Beverly Hills, Sage, 1967), generally referred to as *URS.* This is a computer-produced, annotated bibliography of the "significant literature in the political and behavioral sciences". The main work is subtitled *Political Science, Government and Public Policy Series,* and has 10 volumes, covering international affairs, law, government and public opinion, mass behaviour and political psychology, economic regulation, business and government, public policy and the management of science, and comparative government and cultures. It is updated by the quarterly microfiche cumulations and bound annual supplements, which also cumulate triennially. The aim of the work is to provide a depth-indexing approach to the literature, and it uses descriptors to indicate whether the work cited is a book, a long article, or a short article. It indicates the approach, problem or methodology, and gives basic annotations. *URS* is a highly selective bibliography which is aimed at the needs of the middle group of scholars between the most general public and the highly specialized researcher. Unfortunately it is somewhat cumbersome in use, having indexes only to the individual volumes and not to the work as a whole.

Bibliographie Générale des Sciences Juridiques, Politiques, Economiques et Sociales by A. Grandin (Paris, Recueil Sirey, 1926-51) is a broadly classified series of 22 volumes of monograph publications, primarily in French, with an international scope, being a valuable retrospective bibliography for all the social sciences, but with an emphasis on law.

The American Bibliographical Service issues a series of international subject indexes to current books and other separates under the general title *Quarterly Checklist*, which gives details of new and recent materials in all western languages, and includes reprints, new editions, and translations.

Many University libraries issue detailed bibliographies of their own stocks, which are available to other bodies, and these can serve as useful bibliographies. One such example is the University of Essex Library's *Social and Comparative Studies: a bibliography of the reference material held by the library* (Colchester, UEL, 1969, supplement, 1970), which has useful annotations to many of the items, and is currently being revised and replaced by handbooks for individual subjects.

Some of the larger bookshops also issue catalogues of broad subject areas, such as the Economists' Bookshop Ltd., Clare Market, Portugal Street, London, WC 2, for the social sciences. The latest of these catalogues contains details of some 3000 books, and the same bookseller issues selected reading lists on individual subjects, which include a short introduction by a specialist.

Sociology

The main current bibliography in sociology is the *International Bibliography of Sociology,* which forms part of the *International Bibliography of the Social Sciences,* listing over 6000 items in each volume. An extremely useful series of retrospective bibliographies is carried in *Current Sociology*

(The Hague, Mouton, for UNESCO, 1951- , issued three times a year). Each issue of this journal is devoted to a trend analysis in a specific area of the subject, together with an extensive classified and annotated bibliography. The great advantage that these bibliographies have over most others on the same topics is that they are truly international in scope.

There are a number of special subject bibliographies within sociology, such as John Brode's *The Process of Modernization: an annotated bibliography of the sociocultural aspects of development* (Cambridge, Mass., Harvard University Press, 1969), which gives notes for some of the entries, and stars items from 1 to 3 according to the degree of relevance of the work to an understanding of the process of modernization; and *Mathematical Sociology: a selective annotated bibliography* (London, London School of Economics/ Weidenfeld and Nicholson, 1969), by Janet Holland and M. D. Steiner, or *Bibliography on Methods of Social and Business Research* (London, LSE/ Crosby Lockwood, 1973), which cites 2178 items. Another example is *Survey Research in Comparative Social Change* (Cambridge, Mass., MIT Press, 1969), edited by Frederick W. Frey, Peter Stephenson, and Katherine Archer Smith, which contains some 1600 references with lengthy annotations which give details of research methods used and sample size.

The *Quarterly Bibliography on Cultural Differences* (Sacramento, California State Library, 1964-) lists books, periodical articles, and government publications relating to problems in a multi-ethnic society, but is limited to social issues in the United States. A useful feature is the inclusion of excerpts from the contents lists after each citation.

UNESCO's *International Bibliography of Social and Cultural Anthropology* (The Hague, Mouton, 1958), which is the youngest part of the general *International Bibliography,* is also of value to sociologists in the field of community studies as well as those whose interests lie primarily in social anthropology. The *Population Index* (Princeton University Press, 1935- , issued quarterly), which is an annotated list of books, bibliographies, government publications, statistics, and periodical articles, is arranged alphabetically by broad subject, with geographical and author indexes, is another generally useful tool for all sociologists. There is a cumulation of this work from 1935 to 1968, (Boston, G. K. Hall, 1971), which has over 150,000 entries.

Economics

The field of economics is well covered bibliographically when compared with other social science fields. The major current bibliography of the subject is *International Economics Selections,* Series 1: *New books in economics*

(Pittsburgh University, 1967- , issued quarterly). This series continues work issued from 1954 to 1962 by Johns Hopkins University, as *Economics Library Selections.* . . . The emphasis of the work is on English-language material, but significant foreign publications are included. It is classified, and the brief evaluative annotations, together with information on the type of library and readership, from introductory to advanced, for which each item is most suitable, are extremely useful. The other part of the series, *Economics Selections,* Series 2: *Basic lists in special subjects,* is a series of retrospective bibliographies, the first of which was issued in 1954. It is based on further selections from the selected items in Series 1, but without annotations, as it is intended that anyone who wishes to see further details should refer to the other section. Examples of titles in this series include: *Public Finance, Economic History and the History of Economic Thought,* and *Business Fluctuations.* There is an index to the output of this bibliography for the early years: *Economics Library Selections, Cumulative Bibliography,* Series 1, *1954-62* (New York, Gordon & Breach, 1965), which makes the work easily usable as a retrospective tool.

The *International Bibliography of Economics,* which is another part of UNESCO's four-part series, carries some 9000 items each year, but, like the other parts of the series, the time-lag between the appearance of a book or document and the appearance of the bibliography, makes it of limited use as a current service.

The *Journal of Economic Literature* described in Chapter 5 also has a useful section under the heading "Annotated Listing of New Books" (see Fig. 7A), which gives brief scope notes and short evaluations.

Of more limited scope is the International Association for Research in Income and Wealth's *Bibliography on Income and Wealth* (Cambridge, Bowes & Bowes, 1937-64, 17 vols.). This is a highly selective annotated bibliography of books, pamphlets, and periodical articles in which items are selected for their critical and analytical value. The international coverage is excellent, and its function has been taken over by a journal, *Review of Income and Wealth* (New Haven, Conn., International Association for Research in Income and Wealth, 1966- , issued quarterly).

Other specific subject bibliographies within the field of economics include *The Economics of Under-developed Countries: an annotated reading list* (London, Oxford University Press, 2nd edn., 1959) and *The Economics of Development: an annotated list of books and articles published 1958-1962* (London, Oxford University Press, 1964), both by A. Hazelwood, and de-signed to be used in conjunction with each other. *Bibliography in Economics*

(London, Oxford University Press, 1968) is general in coverage, being designed as a list of basic books for those reading economics degrees at Oxford University, and has nine subject divisions but no annotations. *Methodology of Mathematical Economics and Econometrics* by G. Tintner (University of Chicago Press, 1968) is both advanced and highly specialized, and is an extremely useful bibliography for this rapidly developing subject.

An important retrospective tool is *Bibliography of Economy, 1751-1775* (Cambridge University Press, for the British Academy, 1935), listing 6740 items, arranged chronologically, and subdivided by subject, such as agriculture, shipping, finance, and transport; and for a much wider coverage the *Widener Library Shelflist, 23: Economics* (Cambridge, Mass., Harvard University Press, 1970), which is, as its title implies, a catalogue of the items on the shelves of the Widener Library at Harvard University, and is extremely important, as this library has a rich collection of economics material.

In the field of regional economics, F. E. Ian Hamilton's *Regional Economic Analysis in Britain and the Commonwealth: a bibliographic guide* (London School of Economics and Political Science in association with Weidenfeld & Nicholson, 1969) lists 5117 items (books and periodical articles), providing brief commentaries on the growth of the subject and economic analysis in the various areas covered.

Political Science

The *International Bibliography of Political Science,* another of the International Bibliography of the Social Sciences series, lists some 6000 items each year. It is important that the *Bulletin of the Public Affairs Information Service* mentioned earlier in this chapter is not forgotten by political scientists, as it is of vital importance as a current tool, and the *Universal Reference System,* also described above, in its *Political Science, Government and Public Policy Series,* is with its annual supplements, also a useful work.

The foremost bibliography concerned only with politics is carried in the journal *American Political Science Review* (Washington, American Political Science Association, 1905- , issued quarterly). This serial includes extensive book reviews in each issue, a bibliographical article in a specific area, and has a section headed "Book Notes and Bibliography" which is a classified list of current books (with annotations), articles, and documents. It has a pronounced American bias, but a considerable number of foreign items are included. Linked to the journal is one of the most comprehensive retrospective bibliographies in the field in the form of *Cumulative Index to the American Political Science Review, Volumes 1-57: 1905-1963,* edited by Kenneth

Janda (Evanston, Ill., Northwestern University Press, 1964). This bibliography uses keywords from titles, keeping them in the context in which they occurred, which allows for a detailed subject approach. The work also has author listings.

There are two useful general guides to political science literature: *Political Science: a bibliographical guide to the literature* by Robert B. Harmon (New York, Scarecrow Press, 1965, supplement 1968) and *Guide to Reference Materials in Political Science* by L. R. Wynar (Denver, Colorado Bibliographical Institute, 1965, supplement 1968), which are both biased towards United States publications. Neither claims to be comprehensive, and they can usefully be used together.

A more recent publication is *The Information Sources of Political Science* by Frederick L. Holler (Santa Barbara, Cal., ABC Clio, 1971), which is based on material presented in a one-semester course called "Information and Research Sources in Political Science" at San Fernando Valley State College. It covers directories, dictionaries, and bibliographies, and has useful evaluative annotations, indicating their value to political science researchers.

In narrow areas of political science there are several bibliographies. *International Information Service* (Chicago, Library of International Relations, 1963- , issued quarterly) is a selective guide to national governments and international organizations documents, books and articles on contemporary political, economic, and social developments in all parts of the world. It is useful because it includes bibliographies as well as other reference materials, and gives brief annotations. A forerunner of this service, *World in Focus*, appeared between 1941 and 1951.

The *Monthly List of Books Catalogued in the Library of the United Nations* (New York, United Nations, 1946-) cites selected books relating to questions studied by the organs of the United Nations, listing some 4000 items a year. It specifically excludes the United Nations's own publications, as these are listed in the monthly *United Nations Documents Index* and its cumulations. The work was preceded by a series of the same title, issued by the League of Nations from 1928 to 1945.

Another current bibliography of value to political scientists is contained in *Foreign Affairs* (New York, Council on Foreign Relations, 1927- , issued quarterly), a journal which contains a classified list of new books from a wide range of countries and in a wide range of languages. Seven hundred books are cited each year, and there is a further section in the journal called "Source Material", which is a selective list of official documents and pamphlets, again with international coverage, and citing some 750 items each year. The Council on Foreign Relations has also commissioned a series of retrospective bibliographies based on items which have appeared in the above journal, with the title *Foreign Affairs Bibliography: a selected and annotated list of books on international relations*. So far volumes have appeared for 1919-32; 1932-42; 1942-52; and 1952-62. It is anticipated that the volume for 1962-72 will be issued in 1974 or 1975. Although based on the material which is listed in the journal, each decennial index contains several thousand additional titles, and the latest volume alone contains over 9000 entries and covers thirty languages.

Many books of interest to the political scientist are listed in bibliographies of history, or of constitutional history, such as *English Constitutional History: a select bibliography* by S. B. Chrimes and I. A. Roots (London, Routledge & Kegan Paul, for the Historical Association, 1958), a work with twelve sections, brief annotations, and which specifically limits itself to England. The political scientist will also need to consult *The International Bibliography of Historical Sciences* (London, Oxford University Press, for the International Committee of Historical Sciences, 1926- , issued annually), which is a select, classified list of books relating to political, religious, constitutional, economic, and social history, as well as international relations.

Psychology

Apart from being a social science in its own right, psychology has an important place in sociology, politics, and economics. *Psychological Abstracts* (Lancaster, Pa., American Psychological Association, 1927- , issued monthly) includes new books and articles, with abstracts for each item. It is classified and has detailed author and subject indexes. *L'Année Psychologique* (Paris, Presses Universitaires de France, 1895-) includes critical book reviews, but despite its excellent international coverage, its usefulness is limited as it only appears annually. It is less likely that those working in the field of psychology will need older material, but if such items are required, *Psychological Index* (Princeton, N. J. Psychological Review Co., 1894-1935, issued annually) is a comprehensive listing of publications in all languages, which includes some 5000 titles in each volume. It is classified by subject, and has an author index but no detailed subject index, which makes it rather difficult to use. There are also bibliographies which appear in such journals as *Psychiatry and Social Science Review* (New York, Psychiatry and Social Science Book Center, 1967- , issued monthly).

GUIDES TO BOOKS IN PRINT

Having seen how to find out what books are available on a given subject, how is the social scientist to know which of the items he has selected are still available for purchase? There are two main bibliographies which list works still in print, although these only cover commercially published material. *British Books in Print* (London, Whitaker, 1874- , issued annually) and *Books in Print* (New York, Bowker, 1948- , issued annually), which limits its coverage to United States books. This latter title has a companion publication, *Subject Guide to Books in Print*, also issued annually, which is especially useful as it combines the functions of a subject bibliography and an availability guide, although for a serious literature search it is only of limited use. *Paperbacks in Print* (London, Whitaker, 1960- , issued semi-annually) and *Paperbound Books in Print* (New York, Bowker, 1955- , issued three times yearly) are useful secondary sources, as sometimes a paperback remains in print when a hardbound edition is withdrawn.

It should not, however, be forgotten that even if a required book is not listed in one of these publications, it can almost invariably be obtained on loan through a library, or sometimes through one of the major second-hand book dealers.

CHAPTER 5

Periodicals

The importance of periodical literature for social scientists should not be underestimated. Its main value lies in the fact that it assists the researcher, the academic, and the professional worker in his constant struggle to keep up to date with his ever-expanding subject, although with the constantly increasing number of journals, along with the growth in size of individual titles, it is becoming an impossible task to see even the majority of literature in this one form.

Apart from the fact that information in a journal is likely to be more up to date than information in books (which often take up to two years to appear), journals frequently carry information which is important to researchers but too slight to warrant publication in book form. They also provide reviews of new books, announcements of forthcoming conferences and meetings, carrying reports from those which have already taken place, and often include information of a purely ephemeral nature relating to the day-to-day activities of a professional organization. Many journals also have correspondence columns which, because they provide a forum for discussion, help to promote the interaction of ideas.

Several broad categories of journal exist, differentiated by their particular functions. Journals issued by professional associations and learned societies serve as the media for publishing the significant works of members and other specialists in their field. They usually give an abstract of each article. Such journals publicize the activities of their organizations and record the proceedings at meetings and conferences. Those issued by universities are in many ways similar to the society publications, with some catering primarily for postgraduate readership, others for undergraduates, and all usually publishing original research articles, but some specializing in the publication of translations of significant foreign writings. Periodicals issued by government departments are useful for their information on government policies as well as for a wealth of factual and (one hopes) authoritative information which may not be readily available elsewhere, especially in the case of economic data. Most list current research projects and their results as well as noting new publications. As many appear more frequently than society and academic publications, they are valuable for their currency. The more popular journals issued by the commercial organizations are also of value. Some give digested research results, most carry book reviews, and the articles, whilst being primarily aimed at the interested layman, often provide useful background information, especially for the specialist in one field who wishes to maintain an awareness of developments and current thought in another.

The periodicals described below are intended to be a representative sample of the kinds of journal which are issued in the various fields. Information on where to find comprehensive lists of journals is given later in the chapter.

Social Science

There are relatively few journals which cover the whole of the social sciences, but in recent years there have been several new publications which are attempting to provide an interdisciplinary approach or to cover at least two related subjects.

One of the best established serials in the field is the *International Social Science Journal* (New York, UNESCO, 1949- , issued quarterly). It is truly international in coverage, but it is of only marginal value as a means of keeping up to date with the academic developments within the social sciences as a whole, as each issue is devoted to a particular topic, such as the social science press, history and the social sciences, or the development of the social sciences in particular geographical areas. Its main value lies in the general information it gives about international conferences, social science publications of the United Nations and its agencies, new books, and a section on new periodicals which updates the *Word List of Social Science Periodicals*.

Another journal which gives news of general developments within the social sciences is the *SSRC Newsletter* (London, Social Science Research Council, 1968- , issued irregularly). This serial carries information relating to research and developments in the social sciences, grants awarded for research, new publications, research reports deposited at the BL (Lending Division), and articles of general interest, such as social science resources, or the government's attitude to research in particular areas.

Journals of the more academic type include the *American Behavioral Scientist* (Beverly Hills, Cal., Sage, 1957- , issued bi-monthly). This serial, like many others with general coverage, devotes each issue to a general theme, as, for example, social and political aspects of millenarian and messianic movements; women in the professions; intellectual trends versus fads in directions of international relations; and urban studies, which are all topics discussed in recent issues. The section headed "New Studies" is a useful bibliography, and is described in Chapter 4.

Another journal of an academic nature and devoted to the whole of the social sciences is *Social Praxis* (The Hague, Mouton, 1973- , issued quarterly), which describes itself as being "international and interdisciplinary", and it appears from the first issues to be conforming to that description, and covering the social sciences in a broad sense.

Economy and Society (London, Routledge & Kegan Paul, 1972- , issued quarterly), is an example of one of the new commercial publications of an academic nature which is providing an international forum for scholarship and analysis in two broad social science areas. Each issue contains some four major articles, one of which is generally a translation of an important article by a leading foreign scholar. The reviews the journal publishes are lengthy, and there are also review articles of recent literature in a particular field.

Sociology

The majority of periodicals devoted to sociology take the form of an academic publication, whether they are issued by learned societies or university departments. The *British Journal of Sociology* (London, Routledge & Kegan Paul, for the London School of Economics, 1950- , issued quarterly) is typical of a learned journal in the field. Its scope is sociology in its widest context, including such topics as criminology and welfare. A notable feature is its book-review section. The major societies issue their own journals, for example *Sociology* (London, Oxford University Press, for the British Sociological Association 1967- , issued quarterly), *American Sociological Review* (Washington, American Sociological Association, 1936- , issued bimonthly), and *American Sociologist* (Washington, American Sociological Association, 1965- , issued nine times yearly) being in the form of a newsletter since it merged with *ASA Footnotes* in 1972, which between them cater for all levels of the general readership of the American Sociological Association. In addition this body issued the more specialized *Sociometry* (Washington, American Sociological Association, 1937- , issued quarterly), which is devoted to research in social psychology.

Economics

There are journals of all kinds in the field of economics, although here again there are many which fall into the academic group. There are also many journals issued by government departments, for example *Trade and Industry* (London, HMSO, for the Department of Trade and Industry, 1886- , issued weekly) and *Economic Trends* (London, HMSO, 1953- , issued monthly), both of which provide general information relating to movement in the national economy, and are therefore of vital importance to any economist. Other journals which are of value to economists are the house journals issued by many commercial organizations, aimed primarily at their own employees, but containing information and articles of wider interest, as, for example, the *Midland Bank Review* (London, Midland Bank, 1918- , issued quarterly), which includes a section headed "Government and Business" which lists and briefly describes major policy developments which will have an influence on business and economics. The popular journals aimed at a general readership, like *The Economist* (London, Economist Newspaper Ltd., 1842- , issued weekly), which gives information of a very broad nature, as well as book reviews and useful articles, have the value of up-to-dateness, as they are usually issued weekly, unlike the academic publications.

Political Science

As well as the journals of an academic nature, the political scientist needs to be aware of the more general periodicals which contain opinions and comment, not necessarily written with the political scientist in view, but more likely aimed at the average reader whose interests will be wide. Such serials include the *New Statesman* (London, Statesman and National Publishing Co., 1913- , issued weekly), which describes itself as "an independent political and literary review", the *Spectator* (London, Spectator Ltd., 1828- , issued weekly), the American publications *New Leader* (New York, American Labor Conference on International Affairs, 1927- , issued bi-weekly), and *The Nation* (New York, Nation Co., 1865- , issued weekly).

Psychology

Many periodicals in the field of psychology are intended primarily for social psychologists, and an equally large number are medical journals which specialize in psychiatry, with several others being primarily concerned with social work. It is therefore necessary for the psychologist to examine the other lists in this section and Chapter 9, or the specialist bibliographies of periodicals which are described later in this chapter.

The following list is representative of the more significant journals to be found in the social sciences:

Acta Politica (Mappel, Netherlands, Boom en Zoon, for the Netherlands Political Science Association, 1965- , issued quarterly).

Acta Psychologica (Amsterdam, North-Holland Publishing Co., 1935- , issued monthly).

Acta Sociologica: Scandinavian review of sociology (Copenhagen, Munksgaard, 1955- , issued quarterly), with text in English, French, and German.

African Affairs (London, Royal African Society, 1901- , issued quarterly).

American Anthropologist (Washington, American Anthropological Association, 1888- , issued bi-monthly).

American Economic Review (Evanston, I11., American Economic Association, 1911- , issued five times yearly) contains long and highly specialized articles.

American Economist (New York University, 1963- , issued semi-annually).

American Journal of Psychology (Urbana, University of Illinois Press, 1887- , issued quarterly).

American Journal of Sociology (University of Chicago Press, 1898- , issued bi-monthly).

American Political Science Review (Washington, American Political Science Association, 1906- , issued quarterly).

American Psychologist (Washington, American Psychological Association, 1946- , issued monthly).

American Quarterly (University of Pennsylvania, for the American Studies Association, 1949- , issued quarterly).

Analysis of Current Developments in the Soviet Union (Munich, Institute for the Study of USSR, 1957- , issued weekly).

Annals of the American Academy of Political and Social Sciences (Philadelphia, Pa., The Academy, 1890- , issued bi-monthly), a learned journal with some emphasis on political science but including the broader social science areas.

Annėe Psychologique (Paris, Presses Universitaires de France, 1884- , issued semi-annually). French text with summaries in English.

Applied Economics (Oxford, Pergamon Press, 1969- , issued quarterly).

Archives europēenes de Sociologie (Paris, Librarie Plon, 1960- , issued semi-annually), with text in English, French, and German.

Australian and New Zealand Journal of Sociology (Canberra, Australian National University, 1965- , issued semi-annually).

Australian Journal of Politics and History (Brisbane, University of Queensland Press, 1955- , issued three times yearly).

Australian Journal of Psychology (Parkville, Victoria, Australian Psychological Society, 1949- , issued three times yearly).

Australian Quarterly (Sydney, Australian Institute of Political Science, 1929- , issued quarterly).

British Journal of Educational Psychology (London, Methuen, for the British Psychological Society, 1931- , issued three times yearly).

British Journal of Mathematical and Statistical Psychology (London, British Psychological Society, 1948- , issued semi-annually).

British Journal of Medical Psychology (London, British Psychological Society, 1920- , issued quarterly).

British Journal of Political Science (London, Cambridge University Press, 1971- , issued quarterly).

British Journal of Psychology (London, Cambridge University Press, for the British Psychological Society, 1904 , issued quarterly).

British Journal of Social and Clinical Psychology (Cambridge University Press, for the British Psychological Society, 1962- , issued three times yearly).

Bulletin of the European Communities (Luxembourg, EEC, 1968- , issued monthly).

Business Economics (Washington, National Association of Business Economists, 1965- , issued quarterly).

Canadian Journal of Economics (University of Toronto Press, for the Canadian Economic Association, 1968- , issued quarterly).

Canadian Journal of Political Science (University of Toronto Press, for the Canadian Political Science Association, 1968- , issued quarterly), which supersedes the *Canadian Journal of Economics and Political Science* that was issued from 1935 to 1967.

Canadian Journal of Psychology (University of Toronto Press, for the Canadian Psychological Association, 1947- , issued quarterly).

Canadian Psychologist (Ottawa, Canadian Psychological Association, 1951- , issued quarterly).

Canadian Review of Sociology and Anthropology (Montreal, Canadian Sociology and Anthropology Association, 1964- , issued quarterly).

Ceskoslovenska Psychologie (Prague, Institute of Psychology, 1956- , issued bi-monthly) has some articles in English, most in Czech with English and Russian summaries.

Common Market (The Hague, Herengracht, 1960- , issued monthly) is a review of European integration and economic development.

Comparative Political Studies (Beverly Hills, Calif., Sage, 1968- , issued quarterly).

Comparative Politics (University of Chicago Press, 1968- , issued quarterly).

Comparative Studies in Society and History: an international quarterly (Cambridge University Press, 1958- , issued quarterly).

Congressional Quarterly Service. Weekly Report (Washington, Congressional Quarterly, 1945- , issued weekly) reports on major issues, politics, and forecasts future outcome of present events, as well as recording action on bills introduced in Congress. The service has a *Quarterly Index.*

Constitutional and Parliamentary Information (Geneva, Inter-Parliamentary Union, 1948- , issued quarterly).

Contemporary Psychology (Washington, American Psychological Association, 1956- , issued monthly).

Contemporary Sociology: a journal of reviews (Washington, American Sociological Association, 1972- , issued bi-monthly).

Crossbow (London, Bow Publications, 1957- , issued quarterly) describes itself as being for Britain's younger Conservatives.

Current History (Philadelphia, Pa., Current History Inc., 1914- , issued monthly). International in scope.

Current Sociology/Sociologie Contemporaine (Netherlands, Mouton Co., 1959- , issued three times yearly).

Deutschland Archiv (Cologne, Kiepenheuer und Witsch, 1950- , issued monthly), a West German publication devoted to East German questions and political affairs.

Developmental Psychology (Washington, American Psychological Association, 1969- , issued bi-monthly).

East European Economics (White Plains, NY, International Arts and Sciences Press, 1962- , issued quarterly) contains translations of articles from all the east European countries except the USSR.

East European Quarterly (University of Colorado Press, 1967- , issued quarterly).

Econometrica (Bristol, Arrowsmith, 1933- , issued quarterly).

Economic Age (London, Thomas, 1969- , issued bi-monthly).

Economic Development and Cultural Change (University of Chicago Press, 1952- , issued quarterly).

Economic History Review (Cambridge, Economic History Society, 1927- , issued three times yearly) has annual summaries of periodical literature from and about individual countries, and "Essays in Bibliography and Criticism", which are lengthy review articles.

Economic Indicators (Washington, United States Government Printing Office, for the Council of Economic Advisers, 1948- , issued monthly).

Economic Journal (Cambridge, Royal Economic Society, 1891- , issued quarterly) is one of the major learned society publications in the field.

Economics (London School of Economics and Political Science, 1921- , issued quarterly).

Economics (London, Economics Association, 1948- , issued three times yearly).

Économies et Sociétés (Paris, Presses Universitaires de France, for the Institut de Science Économique Appliqués, 1945- , issued monthly).

Ethics (University of Chicago Press, 1890- , issued quarterly).

European Community (Washington, European Community Information Service, 1954- , issued monthly) contains information on activities of the EEC, illustrated by statistics.

European Economic Review (White Plains, NY, International Arts and Sciences Press, 1969- , issued quarterly) includes translations into English of articles from European countries.

European Trends (London, Economist Intelligence Unit, 1964- , issued quarterly).

Facts (Melbourne, Institute of Public Affairs, 1952- , issued bi-monthly).

Finance and Development (Washington, International Monetary Fund *and* International Bank for Reconstruction and Development, 1964- , issued quarterly).

Financial World (New York, Anderson, 1902- , issued weekly).

Genetic Psychology Monographs (Provincetown, Mass., Journal Press, 1926- , issued quarterly) covers child behviour, animal behaviour, and comparative psychology.

German Economic Review (Stuttgart, Wissenschaftliche Verlagsgellschaft GmbH, 1963- , issued quarterly) contains articles in English on German economic research and current developments in the German economy.

Government and Opposition (London School of Economics and Political Science, 1965- , issued quarterly).

Harvard Business Review (Boston, Mass., Harvard University, 1922- , issued bi-monthly).

Human Context (The Hague, Martinus Nyhoff, 1968- , issued quarterly).

Human Relations (New York, Plenum, 1947- , issued bi-monthly) aims to assist in the integration of the social sciences, but tends to emphasize sociology and social psychology.

Inter-American Economic Affairs (Washington, Inter-American Affairs Press, 1947- , issued quarterly).

International Journal of Comparative Sociology (Toronto, York University, 1960- , issued quarterly).

International Journal of Psychology (Paris, International Union of Psychological Science, 1966- , issued quarterly).

International Journal of Sociometry and Sociatry (New York, Beacon House Inc., 1947- , issued quarterly), with text in English, French, German, and Spanish.

International Review of Applied Psychology (Liverpool University Press, 1952- , issued semi-annually).

Inter-Parliamentary Bulletin (Geneva, Inter-Parliamentary Union, 1921- , issued quarterly).

Investment Bulletin (Great Barrington, Mass., American Institute Counselors, Inc., 1934- , issued semi-monthly).

Jewish Journal of Sociology (London, World Jewish Congress, 1959- , issued semi-annually).

Journal of Abnormal and Clinical Psychology (Washington, American Psychological Association, 1965- , issued bi-monthly).

Journal of Applied Psychology (Washington, American Psychological Association, 1917- , issued bi-monthly).

Journal of Comparative and Physiological Psychology (Washington, American Psychological Association, 1908- , issued monthly).

Journal of Economic History (New York, Economic History Association, 1941- , issued quarterly).

Journal of Economic Studies (Oxford, Pergamon Press, 1966- , issued quarterly) is useful for the translations it includes of significant works from other countries.

Journal of European Studies (London, Seminar Press, 1970- , issued quarterly) is concerned with history, politics, economics, and social institutions in Europe.

Journal of Experimental Analysis of Behavior (Bloomington, Ind., Indiana University, for the Society for the Experimental Analysis of Behavior, 1958- , issued bi-monthly) publishes only original reports of experiments.

Journal of Health and Social Behavior (Washington, American Sociological Association, 1960- , issued quarterly).

Journal of Human Relations (Wilberforce, Ohio, Central State University, 1952- , issued quarterly).

Journal of International Economics (Amsterdam, North-Holland Publishing Co., 1971- , issued quarterly) is primarily concerned with international trade and balance of payments analyses.

Journal of Marriage and the Family (Minneapolis, National Council of Family Relations, 1938- , issued quarterly).

Journal of Modern African Studies (Cambridge University Press, 1963- , issued quarterly).

Journal of Personality (Durham, NC, Duke University Press, 1932- , issued quarterly).

Journal of Personality and Social Psychology (Washington, American Psychological Association, 1965- , issued monthly).

Journal of Political Economy (University of Chicago Press, 1892- , issued bi-monthly).

Journal of Politics (Gainsville, Florida, Southern Political Science Association, 1939- , issued quarterly).

Journal of Psychology (Provincetown, Mass., Journal Press, 1936- , issued bi-monthly).

Journal of Public Economics (Amsterdam, North-Holland Publishing Co., 1972- , issued quarterly), international in scope, and primarily concerned with taxation, fiscal policy, public expenditure planning and control, and social security.

Journal of Social Issues (Ann Arbor, Mich., Society for the Psychological Study of Social Issues, 1945- , issued quarterly).

Journal of Social Psychology (Provincetown, Mass., Journal Press, 1929- , issued bi-monthly).

Kölner Zeitschrift für Soziologie und Sozialpsychologie (Opladen, Westdeutscher Verlag, 1927- , issued quarterly).

Kyklos (Basle, Kyklos-Verlag, 1948- , issued quarterly), international in scope with text in English, French, and German.

Man: Journal of the Royal Anthropological Institute (London, Royal Anthropological Institute, 1966- , issued quarterly).

Manchester School of Economic and Social Studies (Manchester University, 1930- , issued quarterly), which despite its title is concerned basically with economics.

Midwest Journal of Political Science (Wayne State University Press, for the Midwest Political Science Association, 1957- , issued quarterly).

National Institute Economic Review (London, National Institute of Economic and Social Research, 1959- , issued quarterly).

New Society (London, New Science Publications, 1962- , issued quarterly).

New York State Psychologist (New York State Psychological Association, 1948- , issued bi-monthly).

Occupational Psychology (London, National Institute of Industrial Psychology, 1922- , issued quarterly).

OECD Observer (Paris, Organisation for Economic Co-operation and Development, 1962- , issued bi-monthly).

Oxford Economic Papers (London, Oxford University Press, 1938- , issued three times yearly).

Pacific Sociological Review (Beverly Hills, Sage, for the Pacific Sociological Association, 1958- , issued semi-annually).

Papers in Psychology (Belfast, Queen's University, 1967- , issued semi-annually).

Parliamentary Affairs (London, Hansard Society, 1947- , issued quarterly).

Political Quarterly (London, Political Quarterly Publishing Company, 1930- , issued quarterly).

Political Science Newsletter (Washington, American Political Science Association, 1968- , issued quarterly).

Political Science Quarterly (New York, Academy of Political Science, 1886- , issued quarterly).

Political Studies (London, Oxford University Press, for the Political Studies Association of the United Kingdom, 1953- , issued quarterly).

Politische Vierteljahresschrift (Opladen, Westdeutscher-Verlag, for Deutsche Vereiningung für Politische Wissenschaft, 1960- , issued quarterly).

Polity (University of Massachusetts Press, for the Northeastern Political Science Association, 1968- , issued quarterly).

Probleme Economice (Bucharest, Academia RSR, 1948- , issued monthly), with text in Romanian with summaries in English, French, and Russian.

Problems of Economics (White Plains, NY, International Arts and Sciences Press, 1958- , issued monthly) contains English translations of selected articles from Soviet economic journals.

Proceedings of the Academy of Political Science (New York, Academy of Political Science, 1910- , issued quarterly).

Psychological Bulletin (Washington, American Psychological Association, 1904- , issued monthly) reviews research literature and publishes articles on research methodology.

Psychological Review (Washington, American Psychological Association, 1894- , issued bi-monthly).

Psychologie française (Paris, Societé française de Psychologie, 1956- , issued quarterly).

Psychologische Beitrage (Meisenhein/Glan, Verlag Anton Hein, for the Deutsche Gesellschaft für Psychologie, 1953- , issued quarterly).

Public Administration News and Views (Washington, American Society for Public Administration, 1951- , issued bi-monthly).

Public Administration Review (Washington, American Society for Public Administration, 1940- , issued bi-monthly). A cumulative index is published irregularly.

Public Opinion Quarterly (New York, Columbia University Press, 1937- , issued quarterly).

Quarterly Economic Review (London, Economist Intelligence Unit, 1952- , issued quarterly) has 62 editions covering developments in some 130 countries.

Quarterly Journal of Economics (Cambridge, Mass., Harvard University Press, 1886- , issued quarterly).

Quarterly Review of Economics and Business (Urbana, Ill., Bureau of Economic and Business Research, 1961- , issued quarterly).

Quarterly Journal of Experimental Psychology (London, Academic Press for the Experimental Psychology Society, 1948- , issued quarterly).

Race (London, Institute of Race Relations, 1959- , issued quarterly). Emphasis is placed on the UK, Africa, and the USA. There is an annual index which appears in July, with ten-year cumulative indexes.

Race Today (London, Institute of Race Relations, 1968- , issued monthly).

Regional Studies (Pergamon Press, for the Regional Studies Association, 1967- , issued three times yearly). An annual index appears in the last issue of a volume.

Review of Economic Studies (Edinburgh, Oliver & Boyd, 1933- , issued quarterly).

Review of Economics and Statistics (Cambridge, Mass., Harvard University Press, 1919- , issued quarterly).

Revue française de Science Politique (Paris, Presses Universitaires de France, 1951- , issued bi-monthly).

Revue française de Sociologie (Paris, Centre National de la Recherche Scientifiques, Centre d'Études Sociologiques, 1960- , issued five times yearly).

Scottish Journal of Political Economy (Edinburgh, Oliver & Boyd, for the Scottish Economic Society, 1954- , issued three times yearly).

Social and Economic Studies (Jamaica, University of the West Indies, 1952- , issued quarterly).

Social Forces (University of North Carolina Press, 1922- , issued quarterly).

Social Science and Medicine (Oxford, Pergamon, 1967- , issued quarterly).

Social Science Information (The Hague, Mouton & Co., for the International Social Science Council, 1954- , new series 1961- , issued bi-monthly), with text and title in English and French.

Social Science Quarterly (Louisiana, Southwestern Social Sciences Association, 1920- , issued quarterly) is very general in its social science coverage, but emphasizes interdisciplinary techniques and studies.

Social Sciences Today (Moscow, Academy of Sciences of the USSR, 1969- , issued quarterly) aims to disseminate information on current research throughout the social sciences in the USSR, and contains articles and extracts from Soviet publications.

Sociological Analysis and Theory (Beverly Hills, Sage, 1974- , issued three times yearly).

Sociological Methods & Research (Beverly Hills, Sage, 1972- , issued quarterly) is devoted to sociology as an empirical science.

Sociological Quarterly (University of Missouri Press, 1960- , issued quarterly).

Sociological Review (University of Keele, 1908- , issued three times yearly).

Sociologiske Meddelelser (Copenhagen, Sociological Institute, 1952- , issued semi-annually).

Sociology of Work and Occupations (Beverly Hills, Sage, 1974- , issued quarterly).

Southern Economic Journal (University of North Carolina Press, for the Southern Economic Association, 1933- , issued quarterly).

Southern Sociologist (Georgia, Southern Sociological Society, 1968- , issued quarterly).

Soviet Review (White Plains, NY, International Arts and Sciences Press, 1960- , issued quarterly), which is a journal of translations.

Soviet Studies (University of Glasgow Press, 1949- , issued quarterly) constitutes a review of social and economic conditions and institutions in the USSR.

Soziale Welt (Göttingen, Verlag Otto Schwartz and Co., 1949- , issued quarterly).

Teaching Politics: Journal of the Politics Association (London, Longmans, 1972- , issued three times yearly).

Western Economic Journal (Los Angeles, University of California, for the Western Economic Association, 1962- , issued quarterly).

Western Political Quarterly (University of Utah, for the Western Political Science Association, Pacific Northwest Political Science Association, and the Southern California Political Science Association, 1948- , issued quarterly).

Wharton Quarterly (University of Pennsylvania, 1967- , issued quarterly).

Yale Economic Essays (New Haven, Conn., Yale University, 1961- , issued semi-annually) publishes PhD dissertations in economics either completely or in extended summary form.

Yorkshire Bulletin of Economic and Social Research (York University, 1949- , issued semi-annually) is a joint publication of the Departments of Economics of the Universities of Hull, Leeds, Sheffield, and York.

Zeitschrift für experimentelle und angewandte Psychologie (Göttingen, Verlag für Psychologie, 1953- , issued quarterly).

GUIDES TO PERIODICALS

Anyone who requires further details about the many other journals in the social sciences should consult a bibliography of periodicals. One of the most useful and comprehensive of such guides is *Ulrich's International Periodicals Directory* (New York, Bowker, 1932- , issued biennially), as not only is it classified alphabetically by subject, with good cross-references and a detailed index, but it also supplies information about the titles it lists, such as whether book reviews and bibliographies are included, and where the journal is indexed or abstracted. Although the work has better coverage than most others, it is not totally comprehensive, it only includes the significant periodicals in each subject, but it is valuable since material from all over the world is represented. The companion to this work is Ulrich's *Guide to Irregular Serials and Annuals* (New York, Bowker, 1967- , issued biennially), which is also international and interlingual in scope.

A more specialized guide is the *World List of Social Science Periodicals* (Paris, UNESCO, 3rd edn., 1966), which is a comprehensive list of the social science journals from some 150 countries and territories, up to 1964. The arrangement of the guide is primarily by country of origin of the journal, which is not the most convenient, but there is a subject as well as a title index. A large amount of information is given about each title, and a typical issue is described, which is a useful means of indicating the scope of individual items. Now rather out of date, the bibliography is updated in the *International Social Science Journal*, and some libraries subscribe to an updating card service, but a new edition of the guide would be useful.

INDEXING, ABSTRACTING, AND CURRENT-AWARENESS SERVICES

As it is impossible for anyone today to know all there is to know on his subject, or to read all that is written in periodicals, which are constantly growing in size and in number, it is essential that there be means of tracing that which is relevant to any individual's needs and eliminating without examination that which is not. For this reason a whole series of bibliographical tools dealing solely with periodical literature have been established.

There are two main kinds of publication in this field — indexing and abstracting services. Indexing services, as their name implies, analyse the subject content of an article, or occasionally of a whole work, and choose a suitable word or phrase to describe it. Under a specific heading will be listed several items on the same subject together with sufficient bibliographical details for their identification.

There are two different kinds of abstract. Both give information obtained from a periodical article, or occasionally from a report or a book, and — like indexes — they have sufficient bibliographical citations to allow the original to be traced with the minimum of difficulty. The first kind of abstract is called "indicative", and the information it gives is usually fairly short, describing the contents and scope of the original article under consideration. The second kind is called "informative", and, as its name implies, it gives a considerable amount of information. In fact all relevant information is included in informative abstracts, e.g. tables, diagrams, and formulae from the original text are frequently reproduced, and the value of this type of abstract is that in many cases it can obviate the need to read the original article, especially in the case of material of marginal interest, and it is of great value in the case of foreign-language originals or those which cannot easily be located.

Useful though these two methods are, they are still not satisfactory for all purposes, and because they can take some time to appear (often three or four months, sometimes longer in the case of abstracts) they are inadequate for the researcher who needs to keep as up to date as possible with his reading in a particular area, and for this reason other services exist which reproduce the contents pages of current journals, so that the researcher can scan these to see what articles have been published which might be of interest to him. Most such services are published weekly, and are therefore as up to date as is reasonably possible, but as they are usually arranged alphabetically by title of journal, the subject approach is limited, especially in the case of the services with a very broad coverage, and a further difficulty is that frequently the titles of the articles are not wholly indicative of their contents. Selective dissemination of information services (SDI) are being developed in some fields, using computers for both storage and dissemination, whereby individual research workers have a profile of needs which is matched automatically at regular intervals, usually weekly, with a batch of document profiles. Concurrently the computer is used for the production of traditional abstract journals and of less detailed services for rapid scanning by those who wish to maintain a current awareness of the most recently reported research work. Unfortunately in most areas of the social sciences it is difficult to computerize these services as terminology is still unstable, with writers in the same fields using the same word with a different meaning. The fact that the titles of articles in the social sciences are not as clearly descriptive as in the other sciences, also makes automatic indexing very difficult. The identification of a social scientist's bibliographical needs is very difficult, as there is relatively little "hard" literature, and the potential value of the enormous amount of fringe material is difficult to assess. Even the researcher may not be aware of how useful something will be until after he has read it, and often there is spin-off in terms of ideas from an item which in itself may be of little apparent value. For these reasons computerized services in the social sciences are not yet very well developed, although some university libraries are operating limited SDI services for their users.

There are several indexing services which cover the social sciences, and in order to achieve as high a recall of material as possible the researcher would need to consult them all. Most services are selective in the indexing of journals, and only analyse the total contents of a few titles. Thus although one journal may be indexed in several sources, it is possible that any one article may only be cited once (or perhaps not at all, if it were regarded by all the indexers as insignificant). However, as often *any* article on a subject is required, rather than *all*, it is an easy matter to consult one of the more likely sources, and usually several items will be identified. One of the major sources is the *Bulletin of the Public Affairs Information Service* (New York, Public Affairs Information Service, 1915- , issued weekly), of international scope which includes over 1000 periodicals, many of a general nature, and consequently not indexed in other services. This work has been described in detail in Chapter 4. Another major work is *Foreign Language Index* (New York, Public Affairs Information Service, 1973- , issued quarterly), which has retrospective coverage to 1968, and selectively indexes articles which have appeared in French, German, Italian, Portuguese, and Spanish journals. Taken together, the control of articles is very good by these works. The *Social Sciences and Humanities Index* (New York, H. W. Wilson, 1907- , issued quarterly) (Fig. 4), which was previously entitled *International Index*, covers over 200 titles, predominantly from American academic journals, but with a useful coverage of significant foreign material. This work is shortly to be divided into two parts, one for the social sciences and one for the humanities. Together with *British Humanities Index* (London, Library Association, 1915-, issued quarterly) (Fig. 5), which was formerly called the *Subject Index to Periodicals*, and which covers British and Commonwealth journals, plus significant newspaper articles, are adequate for most general purposes, as between them they cover most of the English-language material in the field, and they often usefully supplement the more specialized abstracting services as they include items which may have appeared in an unexpected source, such as a general journal which would not be scanned for an abstracting service.

Other indexing services which can be of value include: the *Reader's Guide to Periodical Literature* (New York, H. W. Wilson Co., 1900- , issued semi-monthly), which supplements the *Social Sciences and Humanities Index* as the 130 journals which are indexed are primarily general and non-technical; *Bibliographie der Sozialwissenschaften* (Gottingen, Vandenhock and Ruprecht, 1905- , issued annually), which lists German periodical articles as well as books; and the *Internationale Bibliographie der Zeitschriftenliteratur aus allen Gebieten des Wissens* (Osnabruck, Felix Dietrich Verlag, 1861- , issued semi-annually), more commonly known as *IBZ*, which indexes both German and other periodical literature, in two main sequences, each arranged alphabetically by subject. The French service, *Bulletin Analytique de*

POLITICAL ethics
Bashing away. Economist 247:11-12 Je 2 '73
Common good as reason for political action.
B. J. Diggs. Ethics 83:283-93 Jl '73
Duty and obligation in the non-ideal world
[review article] J. Feinberg. J Philos 70:
263-75 My 10 '73
Hard luck, Jellicoe—but it served Lambton
right. Economist 248:16 Jl 14 '73
MP's interest; let it go, Ted. Economist 247:
18 Jl 7 '73
Moral values and international politics. K. W.
Thompson. Pol Sci Q 88:368-74 S '73
Political obligation and conceptual analysis.
C. Pateman. Pol Stud 21:199-218 Je '73
Private lives, public scandal. Economist 247:
11-12 My 26 '73
Recovery of civility. F. Mount. Encounter
61:31-43 Jl '73
Three components of political obligation. B.
LeBaron. Can J Pol Sci 6:478-93 S '73
See also
Citizenship
POLITICAL liberty. See Liberty
POLITICAL participation
Public-choice model of political participation.
M. Sproule-Jones and K. D. Hart. Can J
Pol Sci 6:175-94 Je '73
Urbanization and political participation: the
case of Japan. B. M. Richardson. Am Pol
Sci R 67:433-52 Je '73
POLITICAL parties
Intra-party conflict and the decay of ideology.
J. M. Orbell and G. Fougere. J Pol 35:439-58
My '73
Opinion structure of political parties: the
special law of curvilinear disparity. J. D.
May. Pol Stud 21:135-51 Je '73
See also
Communist parties
Political clubs
Political conventions

Canada
One-party dominance and third parties: the
Pinard theory reconsidered. G. White. Can
J Pol Sci 6:399-421 S '73
Third parties in Canada revisited: a re-
joinder and elaboration of the theory of
one-party dominance. M. Pinard. Can J
Pol Sci 6:439-60 S '73
Third parties in Canadian provincial politics.
A. Blais. Can J Pol Sci 6:422-38 S '73

Chile
History
Origins of the politics of inflation in Chile,
1888-1918. T. C. Wright. Hispan Am Hist R
53:239-59 My '73

France
Capitalists? not us. Economist 247:26+ Jl 7
'73

Great Britain
Constituency party autonomy and central
control. D. J. Wilson. Pol Stud 21:167-74
Je '73
History
Conservatives and coalition after the first
World war. D. Close. J Mod Hist 45:240-60
Je '73

India
See also
Dravida munnetra kazhagam

Israel
See also
Communist party (Israel)

Italy
See also
Communist party (Italy)

Japan
See also
Communist party (Japan)

Scotland
See also
Scottish national party

POLITICAL prisoners

Rhodesia
It's still a white world. Economist 247:36+
Ap 14 '73
Long arm of the executive. Economist 247:
34-5 My 5 '73

Vietnam (Republic)
Numbers game [Amnesty report] Economist
248:42-3 Jl 14 '73
POLITICAL psychology
Analyse stratégique du choix d'un candidat
dans une circonscription urbaine. J. Crète.
Can J Pol Sci 6:254-70 Je '73
Rationality and uncertainty at national nom-
inating conventions. E. B. McGregor, jr. J
Pol 35:459-78 My '73
Strange case of relative gratification and po-
tential for political violence: the V-curve
hypothesis. B. N. Grofman and E. N.
Muller. Am Pol Sci R 67:514-39 Je '73
POLITICAL reform
See also
Chartism
Corruption in politics
POLITICAL science
Impending agenda for political philosophy.
G. L. Field. Ethics 83:322-6 Jl '73
On theory of statecraft. J. E. Tashjean. R
Pol 35:375-85 Jl '73
See also
Conservatism
Government, Resistance to
Government ownership
Heads of state
Language and languages—Political aspects
Politics
States, New
Swaziland—Politics and government
Tribal government
History
Great Britain
Charles Lamb and Charles Lloyd as Jacobins
and anti-Jacobins. B. R. Pollin. il Stud
Romant 12:633-47 Sum '73
On anarchism and the real world: William
Godwin and radical England. I. Kramnick.
Am Pol Sci R 61:114-28 Mr '72; Discussion.
66:1316-17; 67:576-7 D '72, Je '73
Thomas Hobbes' theory of taxation. D. Jack-
son. Pol Stud 21:175-82 Je '73
United States
Woodrow Wilson and the study of administra-
tion: a new look at an old essay. R. J. Still-
man, 2d. Am Pol Sci R 67:582-8 Je '73
Mathematical models
Parties as utility maximizers. D. A. Wittman.
Am Pol Sci R 67:490-8 Je '73
Methodology
Culture, political culture, and communist so-
ciety. R. C. Tucker. Pol Sci Q 88:173-90 Je
'73
Public-choice model of political participation.
M. Sproule-Jones and K. D. Hart. Can J
Pol Sci 6:175-94 Je '73
Strange case of relative gratification and po-
tential for political violence: the V-curve
hypothesis. B. N. Grofman and E. N. Muller.
Am Pol Sci R 67:514-39 Je '73
What makes a classic in political theory? M.
Levin. Pol Sci Q 88:462-76 S '73
Statistical methods
Regression analysis and discriminant an-
alysis: an application of R. A. Fisher's
theorem to data in political science. F.
Kort. Am Pol Sci R 67:555-9 Je '73
POLITICAL science research
Bricolage and assorted thoughts on working
in the papers of Supreme court justices. S.
S. Ulmer. J Pol 35:286-310 My '73
POLITICAL scientists
Making of an African political scientist. A.
A. Mazrui. Int Soc Sci J 25 no 1/2:101-16
'73

Fig. 4. *Social Sciences and Humanities Index.* (Reproduced by permission of H. W.
Wilson Co.)

Social Anthropology. see Anthropology, Social
Social Area Change
Structure and meaning: implications for the analysis of social change. M.Joseph Smucker and Anton C. Zijderveld. Brit.J.of Sociology, 21 (Dec 70) p.375-89.refs.
Social Attitudes
Baby, please rock my boat. Christopher Cornford. Ark, 47 (Winter 1970) p.16-17.il.
Social Authority. see Authority, Social
Social Democratic Party
Social Democrats in West Germany's grand coalition. Jack D. Dowell. Political Science, 22 (Jul 70) p.52-65.refs.
Social History: Study and Teaching
Historical happening. Brian Harrison. New Society, (18 Feb 71) p.267-9.
Social Life
Related Headings:
Family
Social Psychology
Related Headings:
Group Psychology
Relationships, Interpersonal
Social Sciences. see Sociology
Social Security: Great Britain
Policing the dole: Social Security officer. Christopher Price. New Statesman, (5 Feb 71) p.175.
Poverty and the budget. New Statesman, (26 Mar 71) p.410.
Scroungers or scapegoats? Michael Meacher. New Statesman, (22 Jan 71) p.105-6.
Social Security: Great Britain
Related Headings:
Strikes and Social Security Benefits
Social Services
Related Headings:
Relief Agencies
Rescue Societies
Social Services: Directories
Through the welfare jungle. John Veit Wilson. New Society, (28 Jan 71) p.153.
Social Services: Great Britain
Don't you sweetheart me.... Alan Cohen. New Society, (28 Jan 71) p.152-3.
In place of the Welfare State. John O'Sullivan. Daily Telegraph, (25 Jan 71) p.10.
Outlining a programme for a comprehensive social policy. Peter Townsend. Times, (12 Mar 71) p.16.
Social policy and the 'good society'. Peter Townsend. Times, (11 Mar 71) p.16.
Taking your choice in welfare. David Donnison. New Society, (14 Jan 71) p.61-2.
Welfare: a rejoinder. Ralph Harris and Arthur Seldon. New Society, (4 Feb 71) p.194.
Will it be all right on the night? Economist, 238 (27 Mar 71) p.26.il.
Social Services: Great Britain
Related Headings:
Family Service Units
Pensions: Great Britain
Social Services: Kuwait
State helps poor to set up in business. Times, (25 Feb 71) p.vi.
Social Services: United States
Do better, do-gooders. Economist, 238 (6 Mar 71) p.60.port.
Social Work
Related Headings:
Marriage Guidance Council
Voluntary Social Work
Social Workers
Casework on call. Mary Loughton. New Society, (25 Mar 71) p.488.
Don't you sweetheart me.... Alan Cohen. New Society, (28 Jan 71) p.152-3.
How to become a social worker. Geoffrey Parkinson. New Society,

Sociologists
Related Headings:
Merton, Robert K
Sociology
Calepin rides again: the French scene. Louis All(52 (Mar 71) p.114-23.
Enter the mini-house. Fred Pooley. Town and C (Dec 70) p.529-32.ils.
Epistemology and sociology. Harry J. Keinzle. 21 (Dec 70) p.413-24.refs.
The family and sociologists. Brian Morris. Hu p.14-15.il.refs.
The kibbutz as welfare state in miniature. Vis(temporary R., 218 (Jan 71) p.1-6.
Modernization theory and the sociological stu Henry Bernstein. J.of Development Studies 60.refs.
The morality of profit: society and busines Spectator, (6 Mar 71) p.312.
Religion and Social work: Diocesan Rescue example. Noel Timms. New Blackfriars, ! 32.refs.
The role of the clergy today: a sociological v Expository Times, 82 (Mar 71) p.164-8.refs.
The social sciences and the work of the Chu development of the study of the sociology Absalom. Expository Times, 82 (Jan 71) p.1(
The sociological definition of religion. Peter L. Times, 82 (Feb 71) p.132-7.refs.
The sociological jail. Donald MacRae. New p.24.
When dogma bites dogma, or the difficult m; Freud. Times Literary Suppt., (8 Jan 71) p.2!
Sociology
Related Headings:
Affluence
Aggression
Aristocracy
Authority, Social
Behaviour (Sociology)
Caste
City Life
Class (Sociology)
Communes
Crime and Criminals
Deviance (Sociology)
Functionalism (Sociology)
Human Rights
Leisure
Motor Cars and Social Life
Myths
Organizations
Permissive Society
Politics
Power (Sociology)
Prestige (Sociology)
Race Relations
Sex
Social Area Change
Structuralism
Value Analysis
Value System (Sociology)
Witchcraft
Sociology: Study and Teaching
History and the sociological perspective in ec Szreter. Univ.of Birmingham Historical J., 1
Sociology and Technology
The sociology of knowledge: art and technolo thall. Studio International, 181 (Feb 71) p.4'
Soft Drinks Industry: Great Britain
How Canada Dry mixed its marketing. Jennif(ment Today, (Nov 70) p.131+.il.

Fig. 5. *British Humanities Index.* (Reproduced by permission of the Library Association.)

Documentation Politique, Économique et Sociale Contemporaine (Paris, Presses Universitaires de France, 1946- , issued eight times yearly) covers articles in over 1000 French and other periodicals in various European languages, but only those which are of recognised academic standing, and has brief annotations for many items, sometimes extending to short abstracts. This service replaces the *Bulletin Bibliographie de Documentation Internationale Contemporaine* which appeared from 1926 to 1940. The *New Studies* section which appears in the *American Behavioral Scientist,* and which is described earlier in this chapter and in Chapter 4, is also useful, as it indexes selected items from some 360 journals, and the *International Bibliography of the Social Sciences,* also described in Chapter 4, should not be overlooked, since — despite its lack of currency — it includes many items which evade the nets of other services.

For retrospective searching the cumulative indexes which most of the above services have are useful, as are the cumulative indexes which have been compiled for many individual titles, e.g. the *Cumulative Index to the American Political Science Review* (Evanston, Ill., Northwest University Press, 1964), which covers 1906-13, and the *American Sociological Review. Cumulative Index, 1936-1960; 1961-1965* (Washington, American Sociological Association, 1961, 1966).

Other indexing services which can sometimes reveal items not listed in the more widely used services include:

Alternative Press Index (Northfield, Minn., Radical Research Center, Carleton College, 1969- , issued quarterly). A service devoted to the contents of the underground press publications, and is of value as a guide to primary materials.

Anthropological Index (London, Royal Anthropological Institute, 1963- , issued quarterly) is based on items added to the library of the Institute.

Australian Public Affairs Information Service (Canberra, National Library of Australia, 1945- , issued monthly).

British Education Index (London, Library Association, 1961- , issued three times yearly).

Business Periodicals Index (New York, H. W. Wilson, 1958- , issued monthly).

Index of Economic Articles in Journals and Collective Volumes (American Economic Association, 1959- , issued annually) is useful for retrospective searching, but of no current value as there is a time lag of two to three years. The coverage of this service is wide, including all aspects of economics — theory and applications. The journals indexed do not appear to have a pronounced American bias; significant foreign-language titles are carried, but only for English-language articles. Similarly, foreign-language books are only indexed where some of their material is in English.

Library Bulletin (London, Department of the Environment, 1972- , issued semi-monthly) is based on the stock of the Department of the Environment Library, covering all aspects of the social sciences as well as science and technology. About 1000 periodicals are covered, and books are included too.

Other indexes which are useful for retrospective searching, but which are no longer issued, or which were specially compiled, include:

Index of Economic Journals (Homewood, Ill., Irwin, for the American Economic Association, 1961-2, 5 vols.).

Poole's Index to Periodical Literature, 1812-1881 (Boston, Houghton, 1891, 2 vols., supplement, 1882-1908, 5 vols.).

Psychological Index (Princeton, NJ, Psychological Review Corporation, 1894-1935, issued annually) indexes some 130 periodicals, as well as listing books, and is subject classified.

There is no single abstracting service for the whole of the social sciences, and the services which cover individual fields are not comprehensive, partly because they would not be economically viable if they were so, partly because there is so much literature to be abstracted that they would not be even as current as they are now, although with the increasing tendency for journals to print author abstracts with each article, this time-lag is being reduced. There is also the considerable overlap between subjects, and therefore if an exhaustive search is necessary it means that several sources need to be checked.

Sociological Abstracts (New York, Sociological Abstracts, 1952- , issued eight times yearly) (Figs. 6A and 6B) is sponsored jointly by the International Sociological Association, the American Sociological Association, the Eastern Sociological Society, and the Midwest Sociological Society, and is arranged under twenty-three broad subject headings, covering all aspects of sociology. Articles from over 100 journals devoted to sociology are abstracted, and over 400 other social science journals from all countries are abstracted where appropriate. The abstracts are generally indicative rather than informative, and rather more than half are supplied by the author or based on the author

sociological abstracts
table of contents

Fig. 6A. *Sociological Abstracts.* (Reproduced by permission of the American Sociological Association and Sociological Abstracts Inc.)

SOCIOLOGY OF KNOWLEDGE 73G5536–G5540

2200 sociology of knowledge
33 sociology of knowledge

73G5536
Aptheker, Herbert (Bryn Mawr Coll, Pa), **Imperialism and Irrationalism**, *Telos*, 1969, 4, Fall, 168–175.

¶ The decline & fall of the US empire & the decay of its soc order is marked by pol'al & intellectual bankruptcy. At the core of the current cultural debasement is irrationalism, marked by the eclipse of reason, the denial of sci, & the repudiation of causation. Contemporary art & literature is characterized by cynicism, sadism, masochism, violence, nihilism & obscurantism. Racism serves as both a source & an expression of irrationalism. In sociol, the technocratic, arithmetic counting methodology tends towards eclipsing reason in an elusive & highly sophisticated form, as does the trend towards eliminating causation —either explicitly, or by avoiding the evaluation of causes, or by affirming an infinitude of causes. Intellectually, the drive towards irrationalism is seen in apocalyptic visions, & insistences on focusing exclusively on the subjective, the sub-conscious, the psychol'al, the existential or non-verbal modes of COMM. In addition, there are publicized attacks on values & ethics as either unknowable or irrelevant to sci. The pol'ly doomed aggression & barbarism of the war waged by the US gov against the Vietnamese people testified to the obsolescence & regression of a structurally parasitic & econ'ly exploitive order. But the alienation, frustration & malaise that prevails today may actually be a sign of health & essential soundness of a pop that increasingly finds it intolerable to accept the deceptive, anti-human & irrational policies of the desparate US Rc. A. Karmen

73G5537
Bahm, Archie J. (U of New Mexico, Albuquerque), **Science Is Not Value-Free**, *Policy Sciences*, 1971, 2, 4, Dec, 391–396.

¶ The sci'fic att involves a willingness to be objective. But many falsely assume additionally that such willingness implies being completely value-free. Actually, sci'fic res is value-saturated. At every step one faces the question, "Which is the best way?" Not only is it better to be than not to be sci'fic, sci'ts believe, but one ought to seek what is best relative to all aspects of sci. Exploration is limited to (1) problems, (2) att, & (3) methods. Even prejudice, which is evil when bias prevents or produces false results, may also be good when it helps produce true conclusions. Do policy sci'ts have special obligations re this issue? Modified HA

73G5538
Baum, Gregory (U of Toronto, Ontario), **Science and Commitment: Historical Truth According to Ernst Troeltsch**, *Philosophy of the Social Sciences*, 1971, 1, 4, Dec, 259–277.

¶ In his major work, DER HISTORISMUS UND SEINE PROBLEME (THE PROBLEMS OF HISTORICISM), Tübingen, 1922, Ernst Troeltsch proposes an understanding of truth in history & soc studies that unites sci & commitment. While the Positivists place the stability of truth in the external world & defend the ideal of objective, value-free sci, while the neo-Kantians place the stability of truth in the transcendental categories of the mind & credit the mind with creating the intelligible world, Ernst Troeltsch in the tradition of historicism places the stability of truth in man's commitment to build a more

in which the object he seeks to know has had a part. The subject knows an historical object when he discovers how the object is present in his own history. The knowledge of the object passes through the subject's own self-understanding, which in turn includes the evaluation of the present culture & a vision of the future. Historical truth in soc sci is an act creating the future society. For Troeltsch this historicism does not lead to a complete relativism of values. While he admits, of course, that the values that elicit commitment are not universal & necessary nor in any way situated beyond the historical process, he holds that the values generated by history are able to overcome it. The guiding light is man's quest for greater intensity of consciousness. The various sets of values in human history are embodiments of this quest for wider consciousness in various historical situations. Modified AA

73G5539
Gastil, R. D. (Battelle Seattle Res Center, Wash), **"Selling Out" and the Sociology of Knowledge**, *Policy Sciences*, 1971, 2, 3, Sum, 271–277.

¶ Personal experience suggests that it is a great oversimplification to assume that those analysts or sci'ts who work on gov sponsored contracts are forced by their personal econ & power interests to make their work conform to the ideology of the military-industr establishment. The belief is expressed here that many enter gov sponsored res programs in order to influence the more hard-line militarists with liberal-minded ideals. The SofK on which this self-interest assumption lies must be supplemented by a culturology of knowledge. In terms of the latter, an important obstacle to good policy analysis for gov comes from the fact that most analysts are heavily influenced by a rather narrow academic & intellectual subculture that makes it difficult for them to understand with sufficient balance the problems that face decisionmakers in the real world. Modified HA

73G5540
Gössler, Klaus, Erkennen als Sozialer Prozess (Cognition as a Social Process), *Deutsche Zeitschrift für Philosophie*, 1972, 20, 5, 517–546. (Ger)

¶ Marxist-Leninist developments in the theory of knowledge are discussed, particularly those in the USSR. A basic question is whether to separate a historical-materialist theory of knowledge from theory based on dialectical materialism. Materialist theory before & after K. Marx is traced in an attempt to clarify this. The problem of knowledge exchange & COMM between 2 opposite forms of society is of particular relevance in this context. Knowledge content, it is asserted, becomes distorted by SE determinant factors under which this knowledge is produced. In a class society the econ'ly & pol'ly dominant class determines cognitive processes in the gathering of knowledge. Those who dominate the material aspects of soc existence also dominate intellectual production. The distribution of knowledge is regulated by who has power of the means of knowledge production, the educ'al structure of the diff classes, & the pol'al power situation. Only under a socialistic ownership of the means of production is an equal distribution of knowledge possible

Fig. 6B. *Sociological Abstracts.* (Reproduced by permission of the American Sociological Association and Sociological Abstracts Inc.)

abstracts which appear with the original article in the journal, which results in a high degree of accuracy in emphasis, and means that the abstracts appear quite quickly after publication of the original article.

There are two significant abstracting services in economics: *Journal of Economic Literature* (Evanston, Ill., American Economic Association, 1963- , issued quarterly) (Figs. 7A, 7B, 7C) and *Economic Abstracts* (The Hague, Martinus-Nijhoff, 1953- , issued semi-monthly). The former was until 1967 called *Journal of Economic Abstracts*, after which it was reorganized to incorporate book reviews and an index to the contents of recent economic journals, as well as selected abstracts, which are generally short, indicative, and cover the contents of some forty journals. There is also an unfortunate time-lag between the appearance of the original article and its appearing in the abstracts'section of this journal. The Dutch publication is not only more up to date, but also covers over 350 journals in English, French, German, and Dutch. This abstracting service is arranged according to the Universal Decimal Classification, and has good subject indexes, as well as annual author and cumulative subject indexes. Its main drawback is that the abstracts themselves are in the language of the original. The service is based on the material acquired by the Netherlands School of Economics and the Dutch Ministry of Social Affairs Library.

A cross-disciplinary service in the field is *World Agricultural Economics and Rural Sociology Abstracts* (Farnham Royal, Bucks., Commonwealth Agricultural Bureaux, 1959- , issued quarterly), which is published in co-operation with the International Association of Agricultural Economists and the International Association of Agricultural Librarians and Documentalists, which has excellent international coverage, and includes some 1000 abstracts in each issue, and has detailed author, subject, and geographical indexes. The French service *Documentation Economique* (Paris, Presses Universitaires de France, 1934- , issued bi-monthly) abstracts articles from over 200 journals, representing the most significant literature of all European countries as well as America and the USSR. The scope of economics is interpreted in its widest sense, but the lack of any index makes the service less effective than it might otherwise be.

Political science is covered by *International Political Science Abstracts* (Oxford, Blackwell, 1950- , issued quarterly), which is prepared by the International Political Science Association with the co-operation of the International Committee for Social Sciences Documentation. Some 150 periodicals are abstracted, and the international coverage is good. The service is classified in six broad groups, and covers all aspects of political science and

Annotated Listing of New Books

**000 General Economics; Theory;
History; Systems**

010 GENERAL ECONOMICS

73–0922

ABDELLA, SAMI M. *Macro-economics: The economic system in operation.* Trenton, N.J.: Rider College, 1972. Pp. 99. Paper.

An introduction to macroeconomics designed as a brief text. Following a five page introductory chapter dealing with the circular flow of economic activity, the remaining seven chapters cover: national income concepts and measurement, income and consumption, money and banking, the Federal Reserve System and monetary policy, government fiscal policy, business cycles, and United States economic growth. No index.

73–0923

CHAMBERLAIN, NEIL W. *The place of business in America's future: A study in social values.* New York: Basic Books, 1973. Pp. vii, 338. $12.50.

Addressed to such questions as "Are America's values changing? If so, why, in what direction, and what difference does it make?" The first twelve chapters consider the concept of social value in its various dimensions; chapters are devoted to such topics as the objective conditions, focal, constitutional, and distributive values, the philosophical validation and the institutionalization of values, and the effects of time, trust, and riposte. Having provided a comprehensive framework for considering the future of American values, the author then devotes two very short concluding chapters to this subject offering three "most likely" possibilities. Index.

73–0924

DAWSON, GEORGE G., ed. *Economic education experiences of enterprising teachers.* A Report Developed from the 1971–72 Entries in The Kazanjian Foundation Awards Program for the Teaching of Economics, Volume 10. New York: Joint Council on Economic Education, 1973. Pp. viii, 120. Paper.

Reports of twenty-one more prize winning experiences which incorporate original and stimulating approaches to the teaching of economic concepts (from primary school through the university). This volume marks the tenth year that

the Kazanjian Foundation has recognized and rewarded innovative teaching in the field of economics. "Index of award entrants whose work is cited in brief form."

73–0925

GREENWALD, DOUGLAS AND ASSOCIATES. *The McGraw-Hill dictionary of modern economics. A handbook of terms and organizations.* Second Edition. New York. Düsseldorf, Johannesburg, Kuala Lumpur, London, Mexico, Montreal, New Delhi, Panama, Rio de Janeiro, Singapore, and Sydney: McGraw-Hill, [1965] 1973. Pp. xii, 792. $19.95.

This revised edition (the first McGraw-Hill Dictionary of Modern Economics was published in 1965) provides simple definitions (of 50 to 400 words) of approximately 1400 modern economic terms, descriptions of 225 agencies and organizations, and references to sources of information and economic data. Includes charts, tables, and diagrams when appropriate. The contributors are Douglas Greenwald, Henry C. F. Arnold, William J. Brown, Lewis I. Koflowitz, Jack L. McCroskey, Guenter H. Mattersdorff, and Edward G. Mayers.

73–0926

KENNEDY, JOHN W. AND OLSEN, ARTHUR R. *Economics: Principles and applications.* Eighth edition. Cincinnati and Brighton, England: South-Western, [1936] 1972. Pp. xii, 611.

This eighth edition of an introduction to economics for high school students focuses on general economics, microeconomics, macroeconomics. The final two units deal with international and domestic economics problems. A set of questions to be discussed introduces each chapter. Review questions, summary, and vocabulary words conclude each chapter. Glossary of economic terms provided. Index.

73–0927

LEVY, FRED D., JR., AND SUFRIN, SIDNEY C. *Basic economics: Analysis of contemporary problems and policies.* New York and London: Harper and Row, 1973. Pp. xxiii, 483. $7.95, paper.

An introductory economics textbook written with much emphasis on policy issues and originally developed for non-economics majors. It is organized in four parts entitled "Techniques of Analysis," "The Stabilization and Growth of

1426

Fig. 7A. *Journal of Economic Literature.* (Reproduced by permission of the American Economic Association.)

Subject Index of Articles in Current Periodicals

This mark • signifies that an abstract of the article appears in the *Journal*.
Refer to the Contents of Current Periodicals section to find the page number.

000 General Economics; Theory; History; Systems

010 GENERAL ECONOMICS

011 General Economics

• ADY, P. On Economic Advice to Developing Countries. *World Devel.*, February 1973, *1*(1–2), pp. 64–75.

AGNATI, A. Dal calcolo dell'opinione nei preclassici all'analisi economica dell'esogeneità. (From the Calculus of Consent in the Preclassics to the Economic Analysis of Exogeneity. With English summary.) *Rivista Int. Sci. Econ. Com.*, February 1973, *20*(2), pp. 153–78.

• ARNDT, H. W. Prestige Economics. *Econ. Rec.*, December 1972, *48*(124), pp. 584–92.

BACH, G. L. An Agenda for Improving the Teaching of Economics. *Amer. Econ. Rev.*, May 1973, *63*(2), pp. 303–08.

• BALOGH, T. AND BALACS, P. Fact and Fancy in International Economic Relations. *World Devel.*, February 1973, *1*(1–2), pp. 76–92.

CODDINGTON, A. Economists and Policy. *Nat. Westminster Bank Quart. Rev.*, February 1973, pp. 59–68.

DECKER, R. L. Success and Attrition Characteristics in Graduate Studies. *J. Econ. Educ.*, Spring 1973, *4*(2), pp. 130–37.

FERNANDEZ, R. A. The Problem of Heroin Addiction and Radical Political Economy. *Amer. Econ. Rev.*, May 1973, *63*(2), pp. 257–62.

FRANKENA, M. AND BHATIA, K. Canadian Contributions to Economics Journals, 1968–72. *Can. J. Econ.*, February 1973, *6*(1), pp. 121–24.

FUSFELD, D. R. Types of Radicalism in American Economics. *Amer. Econ. Rev.*, May 1973, *63*(2), pp. 145–51.

• GRAMM, W. S. Natural Selection in Economic Thought: Ideology, Power, and the Keynesian Counterrevolution. *J. Econ. Issues*, March 1973, *7*(1), pp. 1–27.

HEILBRONER, R. L. Economics as a "Value-Free" Science. *Soc. Res.*, Spring 1973, *40*(1), pp. 129–43.

KELLEY, A. C. Individualizing Instruction through the Use of Technology in Higher Education. *J. Econ. Educ.*, Spring 1973, *4*(2), pp. 77–89.

LEWIS, D. R.; WENTWORTH, D. R. AND ORVIS, C. C. Economics in the Junior Colleges: Terminal or Transfer? *J. Econ. Educ.*, Spring 1973, *4*(2), pp. 100–10.

MARTIN, D. A. Beyond Positive Economics: Toward Moral Philosophy. *Amer. Econ.*, Spring 1973, *17*(1), pp. 60–69.

MIGHELL, R. L. AND LANE, E. Writing and the Economic Researcher. *Agr. Econ. Res.*, January 1973, *25*(1), pp. 15–20.

• MOORE, W. J. The Relative Quality of Graduate Programs in Economics, 1958–1972: Who Published and Who Perished. *Western Econ. J.*, March 1973, *11*(1), pp. 1–23.

MYRDAL, G. How Scientific are the Social Sciences? *Econ. Soc.*, August 1972, *6*(8), pp. 1473–96.

PITKÄNEN, E. Liiketaloustiede ja julkinen talous. (Business Economics and the Public Economy. With English summary.) *Liiketaloudellinen Aikak.*, 1972, *21*(4), pp. 515–26.

• ROHRLICK, G. F. The Potential of Social Ecology for Economic Science. *Rev. Soc. Econ.*, April 1973, *31*(1), pp. 31–39.

ROTHBARD, M. N. Value Implications of Economic Theory. *Amer. Econ.*, Spring 1973 *17*(1), pp. 35–39.

ROTHMAN, M. P. AND SCOTT, J. H. Political Opinions and the TUCE. *J. Econ. Educ.*, Spring 1973, *4*(2), pp. 116–24.

SIEGFRIED, J. J. AND WHITE, K. J. Teaching and Publishing as Determinants of Academic Salaries. *J. Econ. Educ.*, Spring 1973, *4*(2), pp. 90–99.

SIEGFRIED, J. J. AND WHITE, K. J. Financial Rewards to Research and Teaching: A Case Study of Academic Economists. *Amer. Econ. Rev.*, May 1973, *63*(2), pp. 309–15.

SOPER, J. C. Programmed Instruction in Large-Lecture Courses. *J. Econ. Educ.*, Spring 1973, *4*(2), pp. 125–29.

• STEVER, G. Impact of Space on World Devel-

1529

Fig. 7B. *Journal of Economic Literature.* (Reproduced by permission of the American Economic Association.)

Selected Abstracts

000 General Economics; Theory; History; Systems

010 GENERAL ECONOMICS

011 General Economics

ARNDT, H. W.—Prestige Economics

The article asks whether economists have given sufficient attention to "status" or "prestige" as a motive in economic life. It is suggested that prestige is relatively important in primitive societies where the range of goods available for enjoyment is narrow, so that any surplus above minimum needs tends to be used for display, and again in affluent societies as affluence comes up against the satiability of human wants. The article concludes that there may be scope for appealing to, and enlisting for activities favorable to development, some at least of the existing status motives in less developed societies. *Econ. Rec.*, Dec. 1972, 48(124), pp. 584–92 (English). Australian National University.

MOORE, W. J.—The Relative Quality of Graduate Programs in Economics, 1958–1972: Who Published and Who Perished

This paper investigates the relationship between journal article publications and the 1969 American Council on Education (ACE) evaluation of Ph.D. programs in economics. Several alternative publication models for estimating the quality of such programs are estimated and used to rate both the 45 "rated" and the 49 "non-rated" ACE programs. A comparison of the publication rankings of graduate programs with those of the ACE showed that on the basis of publishing performance, widespread differences exist both within and between the various ACE categories of "distinguished," "good," "adequate," and "non-rated." *Western Econ. J.*, March 1973, 11(1), pp. 1–23 (English). University of Houston, Texas.

STEVER, G.—Impact of Space on World Development

This paper discusses the idea of space becoming not just a medium but an exploitable resource. Therefore what is necessary is a space ethic to guide our actions and decisions. It attempts to show how the space ethic can help us identify the proper aims of development and cope with change caused by space activities. It goes on to show how this might work in practice, taking as a test case, remote sensing of the earth's resources by satellite. The paper concludes with some thoughts on how the space ethic can influence the application of earth resources satellite systems to world development. *World Dev.*, Jan.-Feb. 1973, 1(1–2), pp. 116–21 (English).

THEML, V. G. AND GALLIK, D. M.—Teaching the History of Economic Thought in the USSR

The article consists of two parts. The first part outlines the history of teaching of economics and of history of economic thought with particular reference to Moscow University. Reasons for the long neglect of study of history of thought, both Russian and Western, are traced to dogmatic interpretation of Marxism and bias of economists. Modest revival of inter-

1614

international relations. The quarterly subject index cumulates annually, and there is an annual author index. A more specialized service is *International Information Service* (Chicago, Library of International Relations, 1963- , issued quarterly), which was preceded by the *World in Focus* from 1941 to 1951. This is a selective service not limited to periodicals, but covering a wide range of national and international publications, and the abstracts are in the form of short scope notes. All aspects of political, economic, and social developments are covered, but the main emphasis is on the political implications of these developments.

Psychological Abstracts (Washington, American Psychological Association, 1927- , issued monthly) (Fig. 8), is an excellent service which covers over 800 periodicals in English and foreign languages, abstracting all the significant literature in the field, as well as in related disciplines such as social psychology, and cultural and social processes. The aim of the service is to present descriptive summaries rather than evaluative abstracts. The arrangement is under broad subjects, and there are monthly author and subject indexes which cumulate annually. Two other services also include psychology: *Biological Abstracts* (Philadelphia, Pa., Biological Abstracts, 1926- , issued semi-monthly), which covers all the significant scientific journals which include biology, and within that scope, biological, and genetic psychology, throughout the world, and has a subject arrangement with annual and cumulative indexes. The other important service covers medical and clinical aspects of psychology which is *Index Medicus* (Washington, National Library of Medicine, 1960- , issued monthly), a highly developed computerized service arranged alphabetically by subject, allied to which there are several services offered to individual users, notably the automatic compilation of demand bibliographies. The abstracts cover all medical literature in all languages, and psychology and related medical subjects are excellently covered. The service is also remarkably well up to date, and its use is facilitated by the excellent indexes which cumulate annually.

Other abstracting services of use to social scientists include:

Abstracts in Anthropology (Westport, Conn., Greenwood, 1970- , issued quarterly).

Excerpta Medica Section 32: Psychiatry (Amsterdam, Excerpta Medica Foundation, 1948- , issued monthly).

Geographical Abstracts, Sections C and D (Norwich, University of East Anglia, 1966- , issued bi-monthly). These two sections cover economic and social geography respectively.

51: 909–920   *SOCIAL BEHAVIOR AND INTERPERSONAL PROCESSES*

dynamics (e.g., relative professional status) in reaching consensus is discussed.—*A. Olson.*

910. **Weinberg, Martin S. & Rubington, Earl.** (Indiana U., Inst. for Sex Research) **The solution of social problems: Five perspectives.** New York, N.Y.: Oxford U. Press, 1973. ix, 310 p. $3.95.—Presents a sociology textbook which focuses on the 5 theoretical perspectives of social pathology, social disorganization, value conflict, deviant behavior, and labeling. Emphasis is placed on enabling the student to intelligently choose solutions to social problems.

911. **Wogan, Michael & Elliott, James P.** (U. Connecticut, Student Mental Health Service) **Drug use and level of anxiety among college students.** *Journal of Youth & Adolescence,* 1972(Dec), 325–331.—Hypothesized, on the basis of earlier research, that more anxious individuals were more likely to experiment with drugs. However, in an analysis of 55 male and 80 female undergraduate drug users and nonusers, this was not found to be the case. Male drug users and nonusers were not found to differ in mean anxiety score on 3 separate anxiety scales. Female users were found to be less anxious than nonusers. Results are consistent with recent research in suggesting that drug users may be more socially outgoing and adventuresome than nonusers. (19 ref.)—*Journal abstract.*

912. **Zucker, Robert A. & Van Horn, Holly.** (Michigan State U.) **Sibling social structure and oral behavior: Drinking and smoking in adolescence.** *Quarterly Journal of Studies on Alcohol,* 1972(Mar), Vol. 33(1-A), 193–197.—Examined relationships between the quantity and frequency of drinking, problems related to drinking, cigarette smoking, and birth rank and space between siblings in 104 male 16–18 yr olds. The only significant finding was the greater amounts of drinking, problem drinking, and smoking among the firstborn with small gaps between them and the next sibling compared with the firstborn with larger gaps.—*Journal abstract.*

SOCIAL BEHAVIOR AND INTERPERSONAL PROCESSES

913. **Albert, Gerald.** (Long Island U.) **Needed: A rebellion against romance.** *Journal of Family Counseling,* 1973(Win), Vol. 1(1), 28–34.—Criticizes romantic love as a basis for selecting marriage partners. It is proposed that some other method is needed, and that some elements known to be destructive to marital adjustment already have been identified.

914. **Bandura, Albert.** (Stanford U.) **Aggression: A social learning analysis.** Englewood Cliffs, N.J.: Prentice-Hall, 1973. ix, 390 p. $8.95.—Presents a unified conceptual system for understanding both individual and collective violence. The learning of aggression, the processes which trigger violence, and the rewards and punishments of aggression are discussed. Guidelines for reducing societal levels of aggression are presented. (42 p. ref.)

915. **Brammer, Lawrence M.** (U. Washington) **The helping relationship: Process and skills.** Englewood Cliffs, N.J.: Prentice-Hall, 1973. vi, 170 p. $7.95(cloth), $2.95(paper).—Presents a balanced approach to understanding, comforting, and action skills essential for those engaged in the process of helping others. Exercises are included for learning attending, paraphrasing, and desensitization skills. (77 ref.)

916. **Dengerink, H. A. & Levendusky, P. G.** (Washington State U.) **Effects of massive retaliation and balance of power on aggression.** *Journal of Experimental Research in Personality,* 1972(Dec), Vol. 6(2–3), 230–236.—Studied aggression in the form of shock setting by 51 male undergraduates in a competitive reaction task. Group 1 Ss and opponents were permitted to set only moderate shock intensities; Group 2 Ss could set very intense shocks for the other person. An apparent apparatus failure resulted in Group 3 Ss and opponents losing the massive retaliation capacity. In Groups 4 and 5, the massive retaliation capacity failed for either the Ss or opponents, but not for both. All opponent responses were actually controlled by E. Results show that aggression was significantly suppressed only when the opponent was able to deliver more intense shocks than the S.—*Journal abstract.*

917. **Dielman, T. E.; Barton, K. & Cattell, R. B.** (U. Michigan, Inst. for Social Research) **Cross-validational evidence on the structure of parental reports of child-rearing practices.** *Journal of Social Psychology,* 1973(Aug), Vol. 90(2), 243–250.—Administered a child-rearing questionnaire to 331 mothers and 307 fathers of junior high school children. The data were factor analyzed separately for the mothers and fathers and the results compared to those of an earlier study. The factors emerging from the fathers' data were High Use of Reward in Child-Rearing, High Use of Physical Punishment, Promotion of Independence, Preference for Younger Children, Strict Discipline, Low Use of Reasoning, Wife Responsible for Child-Rearing, and Dissatisfaction with Home Life. The factors in the mothers' data were Patriarchal Family Structure, High Use of Physical Punishment, Mother's Lack of Self-Confidence, Promotion of Independence, High Use of Reward in Child-Rearing, Preference for Older Children, and Low Use of Discipline.—*Author abstract.*

918. **Emmet, Dorothy.** (U. Manchester, England) **Function, purpose and powers: Some concepts in the study of individuals and societies.** Philadelphia, Pa.: Temple U. Press, 1972. xxiv, 300 p.—Presents a philosophical discussion of basic social modalities in human relationships: societies, social function, open and closed morality, powers in religious symbols, charismatic power, and vocation.

919. **Evans, Richard I. & Rozelle, Richard M.** (Eds.). (U. Houston) **Social psychology in life.** (2nd ed.) Boston, Mass.: Allyn & Bacon, 1973. xiv, 514 p. $6.95. —Presents a series of readings on the methodological problems of research in real-life settings, examples of participant observation, and experimental manipulations in social psychology. Areas covered include student dissent, black militancy, drug use, communication, group dynamics, helping behavior, and obesity.

920. **Gatton, Michael J. & Nelson, Don A.** (U. North Dakota) **Interpersonal attraction in a role-played interaction.** *Psychological Reports,* 1973(Apr), Vol. 32(2), 627–634.—Conducted an experiment in which 48 male undergraduates interacted with 2 confederates (Cs)

Fig. 8. *Psychological Abstracts.* (Reproduced by permission of the American Psychological Association.)

Historical Abstracts (Santa Barbara, Calif., ABC-Clio, 1955- , issued quarterly) is useful for information on social and economic history.

Hospital Abstracts (London, HMSO, 1961- , issued monthly).

Management Abstracts (London, British Institute of Management, 1960- , issued quarterly).

Personnel and Training Abstracts (London, Anbar Publications, 1961- , issued eight times yearly).

Sociology of Education Abstracts (Oxford, Pergamon Press, 1965- , issued bi-monthly).

Top Management Abstracts (London, Anbar Publications, 1961- , issued eight times yearly). This, with *Personnel and Training Abstracts,* forms part of a larger service, *Anbar Abstracts,* for which there is an overall annual index.

A comprehensive guide to this kind of service is *Abstracting Services* (The Hague, International Federation of Documentation, 2nd edn., 1969), which lists and briefly describes 1500 services in all subjects and all languages.

A different kind of service is the citation index, of which only one exists in the social sciences: *Social Sciences Citation Index* (Philadelphia, Pa., Institute for Scientific Information, 1973- , issued three times yearly), which in its first year is to cite over 75,000 journal articles and monographs, and will cover over 1000 periodicals from the whole field of the social sciences. Citation indexing, as its name implies, uses the references cited at the foot of articles, on the basis that these will be for other items which the author feels are really relevant to his work, and this results in much higher specificity than the more traditional indexing methods, which rely solely on a subject heading. Thus once any article has been identified which is pertinent to a particular piece of research, the user can turn to the *Social Sciences Citation Index* and see who else has cited that work, and which other works have been cited in the same article. The work has a "permuterm" subject index of all key terms in the title of each article which is cited, and a source index, which together with the main volume allow for approaches to be made via cited author, cited reference, organization, subject keyword, and author. Allied to this service is an individualized computer-produced weekly SDI service, which informs social scientists of new articles which are relevant to their research, and a weekly tape service which can be used for retrospective searching and for large-scale dissemination of information services.

Current awareness services which reproduce the contents pages of journals are very useful for those who wish to scan the contents of as wide a range of periodicals as possible. The major service for the whole of the social sciences *is Current Contents: Behavioral, Social and Educational Sciences* (Philadelphia, Pa., Institute for Scientific Information, 1969- , issued weekly), which is broadly classified although some titles appear in unexpected sections, and which covers some 1100 journals from all countries. Allied to the service is the Original Article Tear Sheet service, whereby subscribers can receive "by return" any article which has been listed in the *Current Contents* service.

ABC Pol Sci: advance bibliography of contents: political science and government (Santa Barbara, Calif., ABC Clio, 1969., issued nine times yearly) is a guide to the contents of some 300 journals in advance of their publication dates, which makes the service extremely useful as a current awareness tool. The scope of the service, political science and government, is interpreted in its broadest sense, and extends to such related disciplines as law, sociology, and cultural anthropology, but excludes book reviews, letters to the editor, and other non-academic information from the contents of journals, as these are thought not to be relevant. Each issue has a subject index, a law index, and an author index, all of which cumulate annually.

Economics is well served by *Contents of Recent Economic Journals* (London, Department of Trade and Industry Library, 1971- , issued weekly), which covers some 180 titles, but basically limited to English language publications except for those foreign-language journals which include English-language summaries. Its scope extends to finance, taxation, agriculture, labour, regional and business economics, but it excludes business management and allied subjects, which are covered by *Current Contents in Management* (Manchester Business School, 1972- , issued weekly), which extends its scope into other branches of social science.

LOCATING PERIODICALS

Once the existence of a potentially useful article has been ascertained from indexes, abstracts, or other sources, a problem which can arise is that of obtaining the issue or volume of the journal which contains it. Although most academic and large public libraries maintain files of those periodicals which contain information that is likely to be of permanent value, many smaller libraries can only keep even the most significant journals for a few years because of their lack of storage space. However, even the large libraries do not subscribe to all the periodicals published in the social sciences, as they can only afford to purchase those which represent a balanced coverage. The only libraries which usually buy all the journals on a specific subject are those of the professional and learned societies in that subject area – and even they may rationalize purchases among themselves.

If a library does not have a copy of a desired periodical title it is usually possible for a specific issue to be obtained through an inter-loan scheme, as described in Chapter 3, but often a researcher will want to examine several issues of a particular journal. The most rational way of doing this is to visit a library which has a complete set. Even when several titles are required this does not usually present the problem which might be expected, that of travelling long distances between one library and another: more and more libraries within a limited geographical area are rationalizing their holdings of less-used material, and it is unlikely that anything but the most obscure journal will be unavailable.

There are several directories of the periodical holdings of large numbers of libraries which have been compiled to enable people to locate a particular title in a simple manner rather than having to make a visit or telephone call to all the libraries in the locality or even in the country. In Britain the largest work of this type is the *British Union Catalogue of Periodicals* (London, Butterworths, 1955-61, 5 vols., quarterly supplements), which lists periodicals from all over the world, and in all languages, from the seventeenth century onwards, and states which libraries hold copies. Usually only the larger libraries are quoted, and not all locations are given, especially where the journal is a popular one and likely to be found almost everywhere. Similar directories are compiled on a regional basis by the Library Association, and like the national work they give details of which libraries have which journals, the date at which the file starts, and any omissions from the set. Individual libraries also publish lists of their holdings. In the United States the major listing of periodicals is the *Union List of Serials in Libraries in the United States and Canada* (New York, H. W. Wilson, 3rd edn., 1965, 5 vols.), which lists some 160,000 titles held by almost 1000 libraries. The work is kept up to date by *New Serial Titles* (Washington, Library of Congress, monthly, with annual cumulations), and there are similar regional lists to those of the United Kingdom.

ANNUALS

As well as journals which appear at intervals throughout the year, there are some annual publications which fulfil a rather different function in that some tend to present an overview of the year's development in a particular subject field, while others are entirely devoted to a particular topic, spanning several years.

The contents of such series are usually analysed in the appropriate abstracting journals, but not covered by the indexing tools, and details as to those which exist can be found in *Irregular Serials and Annuals*, mentioned above.

Examples of such works include:

Criminal Justice System Annual (Beverly Hills, Sage, 1972-). Each volume focuses on a specific topic, viz. 1972: The rights of the accused; 1973: Drugs and the criminal justice system. The series is designed to cut across all aspects of the social sciences.

Sociological Methodology (New York, Jossey-Bass, 1969-) is sponsored by the American Sociological Association, and presents information on current research theory and gives guidance on specific problems, e.g. the 1973 volume is basically oriented towards causal models, path analysis, and structural equation models.

Urban Affairs Annual Reviews (Beverly Hills, Sage, 1967-). Each issue is devoted to a particular theme, and the series is aimed primarily at sociologists and political scientists.

A problem which many would-be users of such works frequently encounter is that of locating these publications in libraries, as some libraries treat them as books and classify them with other works on the same subject; others treat them as journals and arrange them in the same way as their other periodical stock, which may be alphabetically by title or in broadly classified order. It is thus necessary to consult both book and periodical catalogues.

CHAPTER 6
Reference Works

ENCYCLOPEDIAS AND DICTIONARIES

Encyclopedias are of value to the social scientist because of the range of information they provide on a breadth of subjects. It is unlikely that the general works such as *Encyclopaedia Britannica* (Chicago, Encyclopaedia Britannica), *Chambers's Encyclopaedia* (London, Oxford University Press), and *Encyclopedia Americana* (New York, Encyclopedia Americana) will yield much information of value to the research worker, although the supplements and year books to such works can be a useful source of information on recent events.

Encyclopedias devoted to the social sciences, being aimed at those who have some subject knowledge, are of greater use, as the articles they contain generally have a certain amount of depth and substance. The social scientist who specializes in one field might well find that the information given in another subject in such a work will be adequate to his requirements.

The two major English-language encyclopedias in the field are *Encyclopedia of the Social Sciences,* edited by Edwin R. A. Seligman (New York, Collier-Macmillan, 8 vols., 1935) and *International Encyclopedia of the Social Sciences,* edited by David L. Sills (New York, Collier-Macmillan, 17 vols., 1968), which was designed to complement the earlier work. Both cover the major social science areas, but Sills's work extends its scope to include interdisciplinary subjects and other subjects which have affected the social sciences. It also updates material in Seligman but does not supersede it. Both works include copious bibliographical information, and together they provide biographical articles on some one thousand people who have contributed to the development of their disciplines.

The most important foreign-language encyclopedia covering the whole of the social sciences is *Handwörterbuch der Staatswissenschaft* (Jena, Fischer, 8 vols. + supplement, 1923-9), which is still important, especially for those

88

whose interest lies in the historical development of a subject. The lengthy, signed articles include bibliographies, and the biographical entries list all the works by, as well as the significant works about, the biographee. This work is supplemented, although not superseded, by *Handwörterbuch der Sozial-wissenschaften* (Stuttgart, Fischer, 14 vols. 1956-65), which again has long, signed articles, many biographies and bibliographies. Another useful work in German is *Staatslexikon: Recht, Wirtschaft, Gesellschaft* (Freiburg IB, Herder, 6th edn., 1959, 9 vols. + 3 supplements), which gives both definitions, historical development of subjects, and biographical information.

Dictionaries are valuable because they help to explain, and to some extent to control, the use of vocabulary, thus indirectly contributing to a more precise and scientific meaning to the language of the social sciences. There are two basic types of mono-lingual dictionary: the encyclopedic and the defining, although many works fall somewhere between the two. Encyclo-pedic dictionaries as well as giving definitions contain information which would be expected in an encyclopedia, such as biographies, discussions about particular terms or concepts, and frequently give bibliographical information to allow further reading in a particular area.

A work of a different nature, and which appears to be quite unique, is *Dictionnaire du Monde Actuel* (Lausanne, Switzerland, Recontre, 1968- , issued annually), which is a card service for subscribers giving abstracts and specially compiled short articles on all aspects of the social sciences, as well as a wide range of other subjects. It is strong in biographical and geographical information. Each card is edge-notched so that the recipient can if he wishes keep his cards in a classified order. Each year the annual volume covers all the items which have appeared. Subscribers are limited to a profile of their own interests, and receive on average some 200 cards per year, as well as the annual volume.

The only dictionary to cover the whole of the social sciences is by Julius Gould and William L. Kolb, *Dictionary of the Social Sciences* (London, Tavistock, 1964). It was compiled under the auspices of UNESCO, and was intended as the first of a series of mono-lingual dictionaries of social science subjects which were to be published with their help. Unfortunately none of the others have materialized. This dictionary is designed to describe and define approximately 1000 basic concepts in the fields of sociology, social anthropology, political science, economics, and social psychology, and aims to select terms which are general and/or in some way basic to the disciplines concerned. It omits words which are unduly technical or which appear to be used only in the analysis of minor or local phenomena, as it was intended that these would be covered in the other works, as well as those terms for which there is no dispute and for which a standard language definition can easily be found. For each term there is a definition, or, where there is disagreement among specialists, the various meanings are given. There is information regarding the history and use of the word together with the sources in which it first appeared; these sources provide useful bibliographical information.

There are several dictionaries for individual subjects. One of the most useful in the field of sociology is *A Dictionary of Sociology*, edited by G. Duncan Mitchell (London, Routledge & Kegan Paul, 1968). It is of the encyclopedic rather than the defining type, and includes useful bibliographical information. Each entry has a short definition, an historical analysis of its uses, followed by helpful cross-references.

A dictionary with similar scope to the one described above is *A Modern Dictionary of Sociology*, edited by George A. and Achilles G. Theodoreson (London, Methuen, 1970), which gives short definitions and has a detailed network of cross-references, but it differs from the other work in that it lacks biographical entries and gives no bibliographical information. A slightly different work is *A Glossary of Sociological Concepts,* compiled by David R. Weeks (Bletchley, Bucks, Open University Press, 1972), which is designed to be used in conjunction with an Open University course. Its purpose is to clarify different usages, to show where terms are used, by quoting from and referring to sociological writings, to indicate where further clarification can be found, and to refer users to related concepts. All the references are to texts which form part of the Open University sociology course or are recommended readings on that course.

There are some excellent dictionaries in the field of economics. One of the most useful, especially for the layman or student, is *Everyman's Dictionary of Economics,* edited by Arthur Seldon and F. G. Pennance (London, Dent, 1965). It is an encyclopedic work which gives concise definitions in everyday language and which is strong in biographical information. To overcome the weaknesses inherent in an alphabetical arrangement it has a series of thirteen related subject indexes to one or more of which the user is referred at the end of each entry. Each of these indexes is followed by a reading list, and there is a general reading list and a list of British journals in the field. A work which gives no more than brief definitions is *A New Dictionary of Economics,* edited by Philip A. S. Taylor (London, Routledge & Kegan Paul, 1966). This is useful because it includes terms which are excluded from the above work and from what is probably the most useful of all the currently available dictionaries of economics, *The McGraw-Hill Dictionary of Modern*

Economics, edited by Douglas Greenwald (New York, McGraw-Hill, 1965). This work gives simple definitions of some 1300 frequently used terms and tries to present both sides in controversial issues. Where necessary, definitions are amplified by charts, tables, or diagrams, and copious references are given to current and original sources of information which provide a more detailed explanation of a term. An unusual feature is the inclusion of a directory section which gives a considerable amount of information on approximately 200 private, public, and non-profit making agencies, associations, and research organizations concerned with economics and marketing. Although a dictionary is not the place one would usually consider using for this type of information, this one is particularly good, as it gives more details than many directories whose sole function is to provide data of this kind.

A more recent work in the field is Alan Gilpin's *Dictionary of Economic Terms* (London, Butterworths, 3rd edn., 1973). It is designed purely as a check-list of definitions, which vary in length from a line to about a page depending on the complexity of the term.

One of the most useful dictionaries in the field of politics is Florence Elliott and Michael Summerskill's *A Dictionary of Politics* (Harmondsworth, Penguin, 6th edn., 1970), which, unlike many dictionaries in the field, has very frequent revisions, and is particularly useful for its up to date information as well as its biographical entries on people who have long since made their contribution to the discipline and its practice. The definitions in this work are generally brief, and, as in most other dictionaries which are alphabetically arranged, there are ample cross-references. Other works in this field include *Dictionary of Political Science,* edited by J. Dunner (Totowa, NJ, Littlefield, Admas, 1970), which covers political terms and concepts, countries, events, and biographies; and a newer work which has excellent international coverage is Walter .'. Laqueur's *A Dictionary of Politics* (London, Weidenfeld & Nicolson, 1971).

Polyglot dictionaries can be of value to the researcher who needs to use foreign-language materials in the course of his work, although in many ways it is preferable to use a mono-lingual dictionary in the language of the work being read, as this will give a more comprehensive ánd contextualized definition than a translation of one term into its equivalent in another language where its meaning may be somewhat different.

One of the most generally useful polyglot dictionaries is *Polec: dictionary of politics and economics* (Berlin, W. de Gruyter, 2nd edn., 1967), which contains a total of about 16,000 entries for French, English, and German words which frequently occur in the academic literature. A brief definition of each word is given in the language of entry, and this is followed by the equivalent word in the other two languages. It is unfortunate that Russian is excluded from this otherwise excellent work. The *Glossary of Economics*, edited by L. Floyd and M. Clifford Vaughan (Amsterdam, Elsevier, 1966), gives French, German, and Russian terms keyed to the main English sequence, and has a separate section on Soviet economic terminology which lists Russian terms with the English, French, and German equivalents in parallel columns. There are no definitions, but despite this weakness the work is particularly useful because of the scope and number of terms listed. The *Systematic Glossary English/French/Spanish/Russian of Selected Economic and Social Terms* (Oxford, Pergamon, 1963, loose leaf), prepared by Isaac Paenson and sponsored by the National Institute of Economic and Social Research, is a classified list of terms together with the definitions and corresponding foreign terms, and is another useful work, although some people dislike a dictionary being arranged in this way.

Up to date bilingual translating dictionaries of the whole of the social sciences or of individual subject areas are unfortunately virtually non-existent with the exception of *Wirtschaftswörterbuch* (Dusseldorf, Econ-Verlag, 2 vols., 1961-2), edited by Reinhart von Eichen, which has English-German and German-English translations. *A Russian-English Dictionary of Social Science Terms,* compiled by R. E. F. Smith (London, Butterworths, in association with Birmingham University, 1962), is a translating dictionary from Russian into English only, and which was intended as an aid for understanding and translating texts in the field, aimed at both the student and the researcher. The emphasis of the work is on economic and political terms, reflecting, the editor claims, the situation in Russian social science vocabulary, although terms from other fields are included, as are some very general terms which would be easily found in general translating dictionaries.

Mono-lingual dictionaries include:

Dictionnaire économique et sociale by Thomas Suavet (Paris, Éditions ouvrieres, 4th edn., 1967).
Dictionnaire de Sociologie (Paris, M. Rivière, 1961).
Das Fischer Lexikon: Enzyklopädie des Wissens (Frankfurt am Main, Fischer) is a series of dictionaries including *Staat und Politik* (vol. 2); *Aussenpolitik* (vol. 7); *Psychologie* (vol. 6); *Wirtschaft* (vol. 8); *Soziologie* (vol. 10); *Anthropologie* (vol. 15). Dietz Verlag in East Germany produce a similar set of volumes in their dictionary series as well as some specialist works such as *Wörterbuch der Marxistisch-Leninstischen Soziologie* (Berlin,

Dietz, 1969) and *Kultur-politisches Wörterbuch* (Berlin, Dietz, 1971). These works tend to be revised as soon as there is a change in political direction, and in themselves might constitute interesting research materials.

For those whose foreign-language knowledge is inadequate for the task of translating material for themselves, there are commercial translation services available, although the fact that they are commercial services means that they are not cheap to use. Nonetheless, there may be occasions when it is necessary for a researcher to avail himself of these facilities, and he can find details of them in *Directory of Technical and Scientific Translators and Services*, compiled by Patricia Millard (London, Crosby Lockwood, 1968), which despite the implicit narrowness of its scope does in fact extend its coverage to the social sciences.

DIRECTORIES AND YEARBOOKS

Directories fall into several categories, but it is unlikely that all social scientists, with the exception of economists, will need to use most of them.

One sort which most researchers might have recourse to use are biographical directories. These are issued by most of the professional organizations in the United States, but it is unusual for the British Associations to do the same, and most merely maintain membership lists, which give no indication of members' specialisms. Those which do give details of their members' field of interest as well as academic qualifications include the American Political Science Association's *Biographical Directory* (Washington, APA, issued annually). Other bodies which publish such directories are listed in Chapter 4.

Commercially published biographical directories can be a useful source of information concerning people who are willing to enter into correspondence with others in their subject area, as the basis of compilation of such works is a questionnaire which is circulated to all those who are known to be qualified in a particular area, or to pursue a particular career. Non-response would seem to indicate a lack of desire to appear in such a work, and might be interpreted as a lack of willingness to confer with or to be approached by others. Directories of this type include *The Academic Who's Who,* which lists university teachers in the British Isles; and *Directory of British Scientists* (London, Benn, 3rd edn., 1966), which although excluding social scientists includes psychologists, statisticians, and mathematicians whose interests could extend to the social sciences, and teachers in schools, colleges, and universities. The problems that the publishers encountered in compiling the latest edition has meant that they decided to discontinue it, and it is now very much out of date. A useful publication in one subject area — and it is unfortunate that there are no similar works for other subjects — is *International Directory of Anthropologists* (Washington, National Research Council, Division of Anthropology, 4th edn., 1966), which includes European and American anthropologists, and is not limited by country of origin of the biographees. Its compilation is based on publications by subject specialists.

Apart from the biographical directories of social scientists, biographical directories of a more general nature can be of value. These include such works as *Dictionary of National Biography* (London, Smith, Elder, 1908-9, and supplements) and *Who's Who* (London, Black, 1849- , issued annually), both of which are principally British; *Dictionary of American Biography* (New York, Scribner, 1928-37, 20 vols. + supplements); *Who's Who in America* (Chicago, Marquis, 1899- , issued biennially); *International Who's Who* (London, Allen & Unwin, 1935- , issued annually); and *Current Biography* (New York, Wilson, 1940- , issued monthly). Further details of these and other similar publications can be found in *Guide to Reference Books* by Constance M. Winchell (Chicago, American Library Association, 8th edn., 1967).

Commerical directories, such as *Kelly's Manufacturers and Merchants Directory* (Kingston-upon-Thames, Kelly's Directories, 1880- , issued annually), which has alphabetical and classified lists, *Kompass Register of British Industry and Commerce* (London, Kompass Register, 1967- , issued annually), and *Thomas' Register of American Manufacturers* (New York, Thomas, 1905- , issued annually) are all useful for commerical information on products and manufacturers. There are also sources of company information such as *Who Owns Whom* (London, Roskill, 1956- , issued annually), which is a directory of parent, associate, and subsidiary companies, and for which there are both British and continental editions; the *Directory of Directors* (London, Skinner, 1880- , issued annually), *Directory of Directors in the City of New York* (New York, Directory of Directors, 1898- , issued annually), and *Poor's Register of Corporations, Directors and Executives* (New York, Standard and Poor's Corporation, 1928- , issued annually), are all examples of directories which give information of a commerical nature. There are many more such directories, and those who have a special interest in this field would be well advised to consult *Guide to Reference Material* by A. J. Walford (London, Library Association, 3rd edn., 1973- , of which at the time of writing only one volume has appeared) and *Guide to Reference*

Books, already cited, as well as B. Klein's *Guide to American Directories* (Englewood Cliffs, NJ, Prentice-Hall, 8th edn., 1972), *Encyclopedia of Business Information Sources* by Paul Wasserman (Detroit, Mich., Gale, 2nd edn., 1970), G. P. Henderson's two complementary works, *Current British Directories* (Beckenham, Kent, CBD Research, 4th edn., 1973) and *Current European Directories* (Beckenham, Kent, CBD Research, 1969), as well as the same author's *European Companies: a guide to source of information* (Beckenham, Kent, CBD Research, 3rd edn., 1972).

Year books as a source of information are valuable because they give condensed data on a wide range of topics. One of the most generally useful of such works is *Whitaker's Almanack* (London, Whitaker, 1868- , issued annually), which includes information on all aspects of Britain, e.g. parliament, lists of MPs and of judges, those in public office, details of local councils, societies, information on education, the churches, reviews of the year in science, literature, drama, films, and sport, and a substantial section of information on the Commonwealth and foreign countries. *The World Almanac and Book of Facts* (New York, World-Telegram, 1868- , issued annually) is a similar publication for the United States, and like Whitaker's work includes many statistics.

Other useful works of the same nature include:

Britain: an official handbook (London, HMSO, 1946- , issued annually), which covers geographic background, social life, government, defence, law, welfare, education, environment, housing, economy, industry, and other aspects of life in Britain.

International Year Book and Statesman's Who's Who (London, Burke's Peerage, 1953-) gives information on international organizations, states of the world, covering their constitution and government, legal systems, population, finance, industry, and commerce, etc., and biographical information on those people who are still active in the fields of politics, international affairs, and commerce.

Statesman's Year Book (London, Macmillan, 1864-), which is strong on statistical information and covers international organizations and individual states. It is one of the most comprehensive and useful works of its kind, and has an exceptionally detailed index which greatly eases its use.

Statistical year books are another valuable source of information for the researcher who is requiring data of a general nature rather than detailed breakdowns of figures on narrow topics for an individual country, and they are useful for the way they present the data in that it is immediately comparable, thus eliminating time-consuming adjustments which would need to be made if data from several individual sources were being simultaneously studied.

One of the most generally useful works of this type is the *United Nations Statistical Yearbook* (New York, United Nations, 1949-). It has twenty-four main sections and gives data on all aspects of over 150 countries and territories. In many instances there is detailed subdivision of topics under a broad heading, especially where the information might otherwise be difficult to obtain. For purposes of comparison a minimum of five earlier annual figures is given. The work was preceded by the *Statistical Yearbook of the League of Nations* (Geneva, League of Nations, 1927-45), which contained a similar range of information. It is complemented by a monthly bulletin. Another useful international publication is the *Statistical Yearbook* (Paris, UNESCO, 1963-), which has a more limited scope than the UN work. It includes data on population, education, and mass media for over 200 countries. *Demographic Yearbook* (New York, United Nations, 1948- , and *World Health Statistics Annual* (Geneva, World Health Organization, 1962-) between them complement the other two works, and these four together provide a considerable volume of data.

Many countries issue series of statistics at annual intervals, and most of these are supplemented by monthly bulletins. Examples include:

Annual Abstract of Statistics (London, HMSO, 1948-), which gives a wide and detailed selection of UK statistics for ten-year periods. It was preceded by *Statistical Abstract of the United Kingdom* (London, HMSO, 1944-7).

Statistical Abstract of the United States (Washington, USGPO, 1878-) is the standard summary of statistics on the social, political, and economic organization of the area. It is particularly useful because it gives not only details of other sources and those from which the data has been culled, but also excellent commentaries.

Statistical Compendium of the Americas (Washington, Pan-American Union and Inter-American Statistical Institute, 1969-) contains selected data, primarily economic, on all members of the Organization of American States, Canada, Guyana, and Jamaica.

Details of other statistical publications are to be found in *How to Find Out About Statistics* by Gillian A. Burrington (Oxford, Pergamon, 1972), which includes a section on the major serial publications of other countries.

CHAPTER 7

Government Publications

GOVERNMENT PUBLICATIONS

The importance of government publications to social scientists should not be underestimated. The British Government issues more items than any other publisher in the United Kingdom and the Commonwealth; the United States Government Printing Office is the largest publisher in the world, issuing over 6 million items annually. Apart from the sheer volume of material, and the fact that there is information on virtually all subjects, government publications are valuable because they are (one hopes) the ultimate in authority and accuracy. Further, a government has legal access to a much wider range of information than any other organization, a fact which adds to the significance of a government's publications, as much of the material produced will be based on data which may not be available elsewhere. Governments frequently publish material which is much more up to date than anything that could be produced by commercial publishers, notable examples being the day-to-day working papers of the various legislatures, discussion papers, reports of committees, policy documents, etc. Other material, such as draft bills, annual reports of government departments, and special reports, all contain material which it is unlikely will have appeared elsewhere, although much of this information is usually well documented and reported elsewhere at a later date.

There are several works which describe in detail the government publications of Great Britain and the United States, the most significant of them being:

OLLÉ, J. G. *An Introduction to British Government Publications* (London, Association of Assistant Librarians, 2nd edn., 1973), giving a lucid description of the different kinds of publications.

PEMBERTON, J. E. *British Official Publications* (Oxford, Pergamon, 1971) describes all the different categories of government publications and attempts to demonstrate their value as sources of information. It abounds with examples.

SCHMECKEBIER, L. F., and EASTIN, R. B. *Government Publications and Their Use* (Washington, Brookings Institution, 2nd edn., 1969) is the most comprehensive guide to current US government publications.

In the light of such works being available the descriptions here will be limited to the types of material which will be potentially of value to social scientists, and examples of specific publications will be by no means exhaustive.

GREAT BRITAIN

The publications of the British Government are usually divided into two broad groups, Parliamentary and Non-parliamentary. Parliamentary publications are those which are required by Parliament in the conduct of its affairs. This category includes the *Journal of the House of Commons* and the *Journal of the House of Lords,* which, being the cumulation of *Votes,* the signed minutes of the proceedings in each House, constitutes the official record of Parliament's activities. (It is commonly thought that *Hansard* fulfils this function, but it is in fact a verbatim account of discussions, debates, etc.); *Division Lists,* which are the records of voting; all Bills, and Acts; Command Papers, which deal with matters that are likely to be the subject of early legislation or on which it is essential that Members be informed. Command Papers include royal commissions, tribunals of inquiry, annual reports of government departments (although not all departments are compelled to produce reports each year, and those which are not Command Papers are non-parliamentary publications), as well as some, though not all, statutory instruments.

The terms White Papers, Green Papers, and Blue Books are sometimes used, and can cause some confusion. These terms initially came into use merely because of the colour of certain publications' covers. Today "White Paper" indicates the broad lines of the legislation a government intends to introduce, "Green Paper" is used to indicate proposals for discussion prior to formalizing government policy. Green Papers may or may not be in the form of parliamentary publications, and not all Green Papers have green covers –

the *Equal Opportunities for Men and Women* (1973) proposals had a white cover. "Blue Books" refer only to the colour of an item's cover (this being for a long time the most popular colour for the covers of all British government publications), although "the Blue Book" is a name frequently given to the annual *National Income and Expenditure*.

Non-parliamentary publications are produced by government departments and other government bodies, such as the Social Science Research Council, for use outside the parliamentary context. This category constitutes the bulk of British official publications, and includes many directories, such as the *Post Office Guide*, reference and year books, such as *Scientific Research in British Universities and Colleges*, and *Britain: an official handbook;* statistical compendia, such as *Annual Statement of the Trade of the United Kingdom* and *Abstract of Regional Statistics;* reports and annual reports of those departments which are not compelled to produce them by command, e.g. the Civil Service Commission Annual Report and that of the General Register Office, Scotland (but not that of the Office of Population Censuses and Surveys, which was formerly the General Register Office for England and Wales); periodicals such as *Trade and Industry,* which is said to be the most widely read journal of the British Government, and *Economic Trends;* and a wide range and large volume of pamphlets on all subjects.

Departments regularly producing material which can be of value to social scientists include:

CENTRAL OFFICE OF INFORMATION.
CENTRAL STATISTICAL OFFICE.
DEPARTMENT OF EDUCATION AND SCIENCE.
DEPARTMENT OF EMPLOYMENT.
DEPARTMENT OF THE ENVIRONMENT, which was formed by the amalgamation of the Departments of Housing and Local Government, Ministry of Transport and Ministry of Public Building and Works.
DEPARTMENT OF HEALTH AND SOCIAL SECURITY.
DEPARTMENT OF TRADE AND INDUSTRY, formed by merging the Board of Trade and the Ministry of Technology.
HOME OFFICE.
INLAND REVENUE.
TREASURY.

Methods of locating their publications are described below.

Bibliographical Control

The most current guide to British Government publications is the *Daily List of Government Publications* issued by HMSO, which includes parliamentary publications, non-parliamentary publications, reprinted items that have new prices, and items sold but not published by HMSO, which includes material issued by individual departments under their own imprints, and significant items issued by inter-government organizations such as the United Nations and the European Community, and a list of statutory instruments. A monthly catalogue, *Government Publications Issued During ...19..* includes all the material, except statutory instruments, which has been included in the *Daily List*, but the parliamentary papers section is followed by a classified list arranged by department or issuing organization, with an index of names, titles, and subjects. The subject approach is very important, as in many cases the dividing line between subjects covered by individual departments is somewhat unclear. For example, because the Home Office section is scanned, it cannot be assumed that all information on say, delinquency, will have been located; material on that subject can appear from the Department of Education and Science, the Medical Research Council, and others.

The Monthly Catalogue, as it is frequently known, cumulates annually as *Catalogue of Government Publications, 19...*, but excludes from the items sold but not published by HMSO section those items which were not issued in the United Kingdom, these being included in a separate list, *International Organisation and Overseas Agencies Publications.* The index to this catalogue cumulates every five years.

As well as the overall catalogue, each Department issues a *Sectional List*, which lists all its publications which are currently in print, as well as some more significant items that it has produced in the past but which are no longer available, these items being identified as such.

For each parliamentary session there is *Sessional Index* to Public Bills, House of Commons Papers, and Command Papers, prepared by the House of Commons Library, and these cumulate into decennial indexes, which in turn have cumulations for fifty-year periods, dating back to 1801. Other useful retrospective works include *Catalogue of Papers... 1731-1800* and *Catalogue of Parliamentary Reports and a Breviate of their Contents, arranged under Heads according to their Subjects, 1696-1834,* which is more commonly found in its 1953 reprint as *Hansard's Catalogue and Breviate of Parliamentary Papers, 1696-1834,* which, in addition to the items that appeared in the original work, has a section on House of Commons and House of Lords Papers. Also of value for the descriptive notes they contain are works by P. and G. Ford under the general heading of *A Breviate of Parliamentary Papers*... (Oxford, Blackwell, 1951-1961), which in three volumes covers the years from 1900 to 1954, and the same authors have also produced *A Select List of British Parliamentary Papers, 1833-1899* (Oxford, Blackwell, 1953).

There are several other retrospective guides to official publications, which are listed in Pemberton's work mentioned above, and it should not be forgotten that many current publications are listed in the *British National Bibliography* (see Chapter 4).

A final note on British government publications concerns chairmen and authors, as many government reports are commonly referred to by their chairmen, and other publications are known primarily by their authors. The HMSO lists generally do not index from this aspect, as the lists are sales catalogues, not bibliographical tools. One publication which can be of use is A. Mary Morgan's *British Government Publications: an index to chairmen and authors, 1941-1966* (London, Library Association in association with Birmingham Public Libraries, 1969), which, although not exhaustive, is nonetheless very useful. Some libraries also include entries in their catalogues for authors and chairmen, but these are, of course, limited to the items which are in their stocks.

At this point it should be noted that there is a system whereby government publications are deposited in certain libraries by HMSO and most of the large public libraries, as, for example, Manchester, Birmingham, and Leeds, are Deposit Libraries, and keep permanently the items which they have received, thus providing useful regional centres for those who wish to have access to the bulk of official publications, although in many cases these collections go back no further than the early part of this century.

Closely linked to official publications are national archives, such as those maintained by the Public Record Office, which was initially established to maintain court records, its scope being later extended to include the administrative records of government departments. The PRO issues guides to its collection in a series of *Public Record Office Handbooks*, e.g. *Records of Interest to Social Scientists, 1919-1939*, which is number 14 in the series, by Brenda Swann and M. Turnbull (London, HMSO, 1971), a broadly classified list, with comments on each type of material. Other useful materials of national interest, including some of official origin, are held in the Department of Manuscripts at the British Library.

UNITED STATES

The US Government is the largest publisher in the world, and most of what has already been said about the scope and nature of British government publications can be applied to those of the United States – only more so.

American government publications are usually considered in three clearly defined groups, which correspond to the three co-ordinate branches of government: Congressional or legislative, judicial, and executive. Congressional publications are roughly equivalent to parliamentary publications, and relate to the work or proceedings of either House or their committees, as well as some executive publications which are duplicated as documents of the House or the Senate. Judicial publications consist of court decisions published by the United States, and despite the regularity and volume they will be ignored in the present context as being specialized and not of general interest to social scientists. Those who wish to have further information on this branch of official publications are referred to Schmeckebier's work mentioned above. Executive publications or departmental series are comparable to British non-parliamentary publications, and as in Britain there is some discrepancy and overlap, some departmental publications appearing as Congressional papers, others as Executive publications.

The main record of the work conducted in the two Houses is the *Congressional Record,* (frequently known as the *Record*), which purports to be, but is not in the strictest terms, a verbatim account of what was discussed, debated, or spoken, in each House. The daily *Record* tends to be more complete than the bound volumes which appear at the end of each session, as the remarks in the sessional publications are edited and revised before the copy is finally sent to the printer. The daily *Record* can be incomplete because a member is allowed to withhold his remarks for revision. Such remarks as are withheld are later published in the appendix to the daily edition. The bound *Record* is also not a purely verbatim account for another reason: it contains many speeches which were not delivered on the floor but which were inserted under the privilege of "leave to print", and there is no way of distinguishing between a speech which was delivered in entirety, one which was started, but for which there was insufficient time to complete, or one where the "speaker" was acknowledged from the chair, but begged leave to have his remarks printed rather than discuss them at that time. Debates of Congress prior to the first appearance of the *Congressional Record* in 1873, have appeared in *Annals of Congress,* 1789-1824, *Register of Debates,* 1824-37, and *Congressional Globe,* 1833-73.

The *Senate Journal* and the *House Journal* include all motions, all action taken and the votes on divisions, though not any speeches or explanatory matter, and the *Senate Journal* includes no proceedings in executive session. These appear separately as the *Executive Journal* several years after their occurrence and by special order of Senate, and in very restricted editions.

Non-congressional publications include a very wide range of materials, such as presidential papers, annual reports such as those of the Housing and Urban Development Department and the Regional Economic Development Office, and *Health, Education and Welfare Trends* issued by the Department of Health, Education, and Welfare, reports of commissions, and of special government bodies, as well as journals such as the *Business Service Checklist,* the *Daily Statement of Treasury,* and the *Social Security Bulletin.*

Departments which regularly issue material of value or interest to social scientists include:

CIVIL RIGHTS COMMISSION.
CIVIL SERVICE COMMISSION.
DEPARTMENT OF COMMERCE, which includes the Bureau of the Census and the Regional Economic Development Office.
DEPARTMENT OF HEALTH, EDUCATION, AND WELFARE.
DEPARTMENT OF HOUSING AND URBAN DEVELOPMENT.
DEPARTMENT OF JUSTICE.
DEPARTMENT OF LABOR, which includes the Bureau of Labor Statistics.
DEPARTMENT OF THE TREASURY.
FEDERAL TRADE COMMISSION.
INTERSTATE COMMERCE COMMISSION.
NATIONAL LABOR RELATIONS BOARD.
NATIONAL SCIENCE FOUNDATION.
UNITED STATES INFORMATION AGENCY.

Bibliographical Control

The current catalogues issued by the United States Government Printing Office are comprehensive guides to American government publications. The *Monthly Catalog of United States Government Publications* has appeared under several titles since 1895. It is arranged alphabetically by the name of the bureau which issues the material. Although most of the material is published on behalf of the various bureaux by the United States Government Printing Office, some material is issued by the individual offices direct, and sometimes this material is not notified to the USGPO, and therefore the *Monthly Catalog* is not always as complete as it should be. There are subject indexes in each issue and at the end of each year. A useful work which supplements past volumes of this work are the *Cumulative Personal Author Indexes for the "Monthly Catalog"* (Ann Arbor, Mich., Perian, 1969, 3 vols.), which is the only author approach to official publications which were listed in the *Monthly Catalog* from 1941 to 1965.

Another monthly publication is the *Congressional Information Service,* which has been issued by the USGPO monthly since 1970. This service indexes and abstracts almost every document issued by or relating to Congress, with the exception of the *Congressional Record,* which has its own index, and its purpose is to enable users "to locate a hearing or report even if all you know is the name of the subcommittee chairman . . . " (USGPO).

Publications which emanate at State level are listed in *Monthly Checklist of State Publications,* which is compiled in the Library of Congress, and has been issued since 1910. It is arranged alphabetically by State, and is limited to those publications which are received by the Library of Congress (LC), although very little which is of more than ephemeral value is not deposited at the LC. The annual index refers to titles and contents notes, thereby providing a useful subject approach.

Guides to retrospective materials are issued by the Superintendent of Documents. More detailed is the *Catalog of the Public Documents of Congress and all Departments of the Government of the United States . . . ,* popularly known as the *Document Catalog,* which covers material up to 1940; information from that date being contained only in the *Monthly Catalog.*

Other useful retrospective bibliographies which the USGPO have issued include *Public Documents of the First Fourteen Congresses, 1789-1817,* compiled by Adolphus W. Greely, and Benjamin P. Poore's *Descriptive Catalog of the Government Publications of the United States, September 5, 1774 – March 4, 1881,* which is a chronological index including a brief abstract of each item as well as name and subject indexes.

Intergovernment organizations

Intergovernment organizations issue large numbers of publications although many of these for reasons of non-availability, or because they are not issued in English, or relate primarily to the internal working of the organization, do not find their way into any but the largest libraries in Britain or the United States.

The intergovernment organization which is most well represented in libraries, and which produces more material in the social sciences in its widest sense, than any other is the United Nations and its agencies. Material issued by the UN is on all subjects, and includes periodicals such as the *International Social Science Journal,* statistical compilations such as the *United Nations Statistical Yearbook,* and the bibliographies covered in Chapter 4. The various specialized agencies of the UN, such as the United Nations Educational, Scientific and Cultural Organization (UNESCO), Food and Agriculture Organization (FAO), and the World Health Organization (WHO) all produce material of this type which can be of value to social scientists, and all issue reports which are of wide interest. The main source of information on these publications is the *UN Documents Index,* which has appeared monthly since 1950, which includes publications of the Agencies as well as of the main organization, and is arranged by issuing body or division. The period 1946-50 is covered by the *Checklist of UN Documents.* Each Agency also issues its own catalogue at intervals, but not in the form of a current guide.

Other organizations which produce material of interest to social scientists include the European Communities and its subsidiary organizations, such as the European Economic Community (EEC) which, like the other bodies, issue reports, statistics, and journals. These are documented, as are those of other international bodies in the *Daily List* mentioned above, where they are regarded as of significance, and in the publications of the *European Communities Catalogue,* which appears at approximately quarterly intervals.

International bodies which are of particular use to economists include the Organization for Economic Co-operation and Development (OECD), the successor of the Organization for European Economic Co-operation (OEEC), which produces several reports, as well as statistical material, the European Free Trade Association (EFTA), and the Organization of American States (OAS), which produces large numbers of statistics and other economic information relating to the OAS member countries. Details of its publications are given in an annual catalogue.

Details of all intergovernment bodies and their publications are to be found in the *Yearbook of International Organizations* which is described in Chapter 3.

CHAPTER 8

Research

Research in the social sciences is growing as rapidly as in any other field, and even those social scientists not currently engaged in their own research may find it useful from time to time to know what is being done in their particular field of interest. Whilst unlike in the pure and applied sciences duplication of research effort can be fruitful, as no two projects will be alike in every respect, it is valuable to know at the outset of any piece of new work what has already been completed or what is currently being done in the same field. This can not only save time, effort, and money, but it can also avoid disappointment should something of greater dimensions and prestige or value than one's own be produced.

FINDING RESEARCH IN PROGRESS

The major source of information on research in progress in the United Kingdom is *Scientific Research in British Universities and Colleges,* Volume III: *The social sciences* (London, Department of Education and Science and the British Council, 1967- , issued annually). The scope of this work extends to cover research being undertaken in government departments and other institutions, such as research organizations. The information in each entry covers title of the project, its scope, its anticipated date of completion, names of the people involved, in some instances publications or interim reports which have appeared as a result of work already completed are listed, and the name of the body supporting it financially is given. One serious drawback to the value of this work for anyone wanting information on research into a particular subject is its arrangement, which is primarily by broad subject, with some further, though not very detailed subject divisions (economics, for example, has twelve subject divisions), which are then arranged alphabetically by the name of the institution where the research is being conducted.

Combined with a lack of a really detailed subject index this makes searching the guide rather time-consuming. The problem is not, however, confined to this guide: most such directories lack a specific subject approach.

The above work is up-dated in the *Social Science Research Council Newsletter* (London, SSRC, 1966- , issued quarterly) (Figs. 9A and 9B), which in each issue lists new SSRC grants, again by name of institution, giving the title of the project, names of the investigators, the amount of the grant, and the period it is to cover. Those requiring further information are invited to contact the investigators direct. This section is followed by a similar one on grants for research awarded by other organizations, this time being arranged primarily by awarding body and subdivided by name of the institution receiving the grant.

Information from the *SSRC Newsletter* cumulates in *Research Supported by the SSRC* (London, SSRC 1967- , issued annually). This work gives greater detail about the projects, and cites publications such as journal articles on interim reports resulting from the research in progress. As its title implies, it excludes research supported by other bodies.

Other organizations also issue lists of research. For example, the Centre for Environmental Studies publishes an annual list of research grants they have awarded; so, too, does the Nuffield Foundation in its annual reports. Certainly all grant-awarding bodies maintain such a list, but it is usually unnecessary to consult these, as the purpose of the CES guide is to list all those projects for which grants have been awarded.

The professional and research associations as well as government departments usually maintain or publish research registers. These can supplement the major guides as they generally include research which is being undertaken during the course of normal work and for which no grant has therefore been awarded. These tend, of course, to be of more limited scope than other projects, but they can yield useful information or can be precursors of major projects. Examples of this type of guide include:

DEPARTMENT OF EMPLOYMENT. Training Research Register.
HOME OFFICE. *Prison Department.* List of Research.
HOME OFFICE. *Research Unit and Statistical Division.* Summary of research supported by grant.
INSTITUTE OF RACE RELATIONS. Register of Research on Commonwealth Immigrants in Britain.
ROYAL INSTITUTE OF PUBLIC ADMINISTRATION. Register of Research in Political Science.

SSRC Newsletter 20, Octob

Completed research and recent grants

Reports from SSRC projects

When research on an SSRC grant is completed a report is lodged at the British Library Lending Division (BLL) (formerly the National Lending Library) so that it is available to others. Reports lodged at the BLL are noted regularly in the *SSRC Newsletter.* They may be borrowed through librarians.

The list contains all the reports lodged in the BLL since *Newsletter 19,* June 1973. They are listed here alphabetically under the investigators' names. Please quote reference number when borrowing report.

Alexander, Professor K J W
American investment in Scotland (HR 562)

Archibald, Professor G C
Excess demand for labour unemployment, and the Phillips Curve: A theoretical and empirical study (HR 594)

Donaldson, Dr M C
Cognitive development in pre-school children: The comprehension of quantifiers (HR 1491)

Douglas, Professor M M
Social constraints on agricultural innovation in a mountain community in Tanzania (HR 321)

Fraser, Dr W H
Trade unionism in Scotland 1824-97 (HR 1107)

Friend, J K
Public planning: the inter-corporate dimension (HR 903)

Harrison, A
1,000 farm random sample survey of farming's business, financial and investment structure (HR 826)

Kirk, Professor J H
Retail stall markets in Great Britain (HR 1080)

Matthews, Dr W A
Factors affecting the short term free recall of verbal ↿ (HR 816)

Miles, Dr H B
Some correlates of academic performance of pupils in ary schools (HR 469)

Millar, Dr S
The development of haptic-visual performance as a f of stimulus and delay conditions (HR 690)

Pinder, J H M
Accessibility and choice as quantifiable variables in I planning (HR 1034)

Robinson, Dr W P
The question-answer exchange between mothers anɹ children (HR 1572)

Schaffer, Professor H R
The development of selective behaviour in infancy (I

Stanyer, J
Local elections in Devon 1945-68 (HR 317)

Thomson, Dr A W J
An examination of grievance procedures below the the company (HR 1046)

Twyman, Dr M L and Singer, B R
An investigation into some aspects of the illustratioɪ mary school books (HR 925)

Walker, R
Towards a sociography of classrooms (HR 896 and

Whitmarsh, G W
Society and the school curriculum: the Association ↿ cation in Citizenship 1934-57 (HR 1096)

New SSRC grants

This list contains the grants made since those announced in *Newsletter 19,* June 1973. For further information, please contact investigators direct. (Details of grants are now shown in the following order: university or institution; title; department; centre etc; investigator(s); grant and grant periods).

Aberystwyth, University College

Bradford University

The use of input-output tables to model the growth in developing countries. Social Sciences (Professor J tomley) — £500 over 1yr

The structure of work organizations across societies. ization Analysis Research Unit (Professor D J Hi — £3,950 over 1yr

Durham University

Fig. 9A. *Social Science Research Council Newsletter.* (Reproduced by permission of the Social Science Research Council.)

Royal United Services Institute for Defence Studies

Concepts of civil-military relations in Europe. (J D Vowles) — £1,680 over 6mths

Scottish Council for Research in Education

A study of language, education and employment in Glasgow. (Dr R K S Macauley) — £2,483 over 6mths

Sussex University

The mental lexicon and the process of comprehension. Experimental Psychology Laboratory (Dr P N Johnson-Laird) — £14,436 over 3yrs

Cognitive development of Yoruba children. School of African and Asian Studies (Dr B B Lloyd) — £2,850 over 6mths

British industrial structures in the context of European integration. Centre for Contemporary European Studies (Professor C T Saunders) — £22,807 over 2 yrs

Swansea, University College

A study of permanent and temporary island migrants in Athens. Sociology and Anthropology (Dr M E Kenna) —

£1,049 over 8mths

System Research Ltd

Applications and developments of a theory of learn teaching. (Professor A G S Pask) — £19,722 over 1yr

Trade Policy Research Centre

Non-tariff agricultural restrictions in international tra J S Hillman) — £1,704 over 9mths

York University

Growth, entrepreneurship and capital formation in bicycle and related industries 1870-1939. Economics a lated Studies (A E Harrison) — £240 over 4mths

A calendar for economic and social historians of exc bills and answers 1660-1714. History (Dr D W Jones) over 1 yr

A sociolinguistic investigation of stylistic variation in hili speaking community in Kenya. Language (Miss J sell) — £406 over 1 yr

Grants by other organizations

These lists contain recent grants for social science research awarded by other organizations.

British Academy

Burlington House, Piccadilly, London W1

Cambridge University

A study of Yugoslav government in World War II. Slavonic Studies Library (K S Pavlowitch) — £300

Cardiff, University College and Newcastle upon Tyne University

A computer analysis of 18th century poll books. Computing centre (Dr W A Gray) and History (Dr W A Speck) — £350

Historic Towns Trust

An historical atlas of town plans — £1,500

London School of Economics

Reference volume on Victorian political history. Library (C P

Department of Employment

7-8 St Martins Place, London WC2N 4JH

Aberdeen University

Wage rounds (Professor D MacKay) — £11,000 over 2

Hull University

The presentation of fault diagnostic information fo tions and training. Psychology (K Duncan) — £2,992 c

Institute of Manpower Studies

The utilization of qualified manpower (A G Atkinson Purkiss) — £14,000 over 9mths

Centre for Environmental Studies

5 Cambridge Terrace, Regent's Park, London NW1 4J

Fig. 9B. *Social Science Research Council Newsletter.* (Reproduced by permission of the Social Science Research Council.)

A list of associations and research bodies is to be found in Chapter 3.

The United States is less well endowed with guides to current social science research than is Great Britain. The major general source of such information is issued by the United States National Science Foundation, with the title *Grants and Awards for the Fiscal Year . . .* (Washington, USGPO, 1965- ,), and is limited for official support. Other government departments also issue lists of current officially sponsored research or undertaken research, such as the US Children's Bureau's *Research Relating to Children* (Washington, USGPO, 1952- , issued annually).

Some professional organizations maintain registers of on-going research, although the American Sociological Association is the only such body to issue a directory of this type, under the title *Current Sociological Research* (Washington, ASA, 1953- , issued annually).

The lack of specific guides to current research is not, however, the major problem it might at first seem to be, as the American journals are strong in reporting new work in their subject field, and it is more common for interim results to be published in this medium than it is in the United Kingdom. Significant journals are listed in Chapter 5.

GRANTS FOR RESEARCH

Apart from the research grants awarded by governments, a great deal of research is funded by specialists organizations and by industry.

In Great Britain the majority of government grants are made by the Social Science Research Council, although other departments which have an interest in the social sciences also finance a substantial amount of research in their particular area of specialization, such as the Department of Employment, the Department of the Environment, the Department of Health and Social Security, and the Home Office.

Other organizations which give financial support to research projects include the Ford Foundation, the Frederick Soddy Trust, the Leverhulme Trust Fund, and the Nuffield Foundation. A comprehensive guide to such bodies is *Directory of Grant Making Trusts* (London, National Council of Services, Charities Aid Fund, 2nd edn., 1971), which, as well as including the major organizations such as those already mentioned, also lists those bodies which give small grants for people from a particular geographical area. It includes industrial organizations, such as Lever Brothers and ICI, and those bodies whose sole purpose is to sponsor research.

The United States Government also gives a considerable number of awards for research purposes, as, for example, the Department of Health, Education, and Welfare, the Department of Commerce, and the Department of Labor. The most comprehensive source of information relating to such grant-awarding organizations as the Russell Sage Foundation and the Social Science Research Council (a non-government body, not to be confused with the British SSRC), is the *Foundation Directory* (University of Chicago Press, 4th edn., 1971). This guide lists over 6000 bodies which financially support research. It is usefully supplemented by *Grant Data Quarterly* (Los Angeles, Academic Media, 1967- ,), which is a journal devoted to the collection and dissemination of grant opportunities and information.

RESEARCH REPORTS

Whilst many results of research will appear in condensed form in journals and in revised form in books, a great deal of information is only given in the actual research report. It is therefore useful for researchers working in a field which has already been covered to see for themselves the fullest information available.

Reports resulting from SSRC supported projects are lodged at the British Library Lending Division (BLL) from which they can be borrowed through the Inter-library Lending scheme. They are listed in the *BLL Announcement Bulletin* (Boston Spa, Yorkshire, BLL, 1973- , issued monthly), which was formerly the *NLL Announcement Bulletin,* and in the *Social Science Research Council Newsletter.* The former also lists some reports resulting from research sponsored by other bodies. Unfortunately, however, this is not a comprehensive list of such reports, and there is no other service covering this type of material. It is therefore necessary for those wanting access to unpublished reports to write to the individual compilers, relying on information in journals and that given in back copies of the guides to research in progress, notably *Scientific Research in British Universities and Colleges,* and its forerunner which was compiled by the Warren Spring Laboratory, *Register of Research in the Human Sciences* (London, HMSO, 1962-5, issued irregularly), covering the period from 1959 to 1965.

Results of government-sponsored research in the United States are reported in *Government Reports Announcements* (US Department of Commerce, National Technical Information Service, 1973- , issued semi-monthly). This work, which succeeds *United States Government Research and Develop-*

ment Reports, is not confined to the social sciences, but as the *BLL
Announcement Bulletin* relevant material is to be found under the heading
"Behavioral and Social Sciences". *GRA* is particularly useful because of the
short abstracts which are given for each entry. A separate but detailed subject
index is issued concurrently, and with cumulations, under the title *Government Reports Index.* The majority of reports listed in *GRA* are available from
the Clearinghouse for Federal Scientific and Technical Information and from
the BLL.

Research sponsored by other organizations is, as in Britain, badly documented, and here again it is necessary for would-be report readers to rely on
ad hoc methods of gaining access to this information, usually by means of
notices in journals or by word of mouth. A notable exception to this lack of
bibliographical coverage is the Rand Corporation's *Selected Rand Abstracts*
(Santa Monica, Calif., Rand Corporation, 1963- , issued quarterly). This series
is a guide to the Corporation's own research reports, the majority of which
are in the field of economics and management. Most other research organizations in the United States and the United Kingdom publish the results of their
own projects, and these are frequently listed in the bibliographies described in
Chapter 4.

THESES

As postgraduate work in the universities has been growing at a
considerable pace during the past ten years there has been a not unexpected
growth in the number of master's and doctoral dissertations in the social
sciences. Some of these are issued commercially some time after their sub-
mission, and usually in much amended form; most are not. Theses are deposited in the library of the awarding institution, or in the case of the Council
for National Academic Awards degrees, of the institution where the candidate
was a registered student, and most libraries maintain a catalogue of the theses
they hold. Some, such as Cambridge University, publish these.

The major source of information on theses for the United Kingdom is
*Index to Theses Accepted for Higher Degrees in the Universities of Great
Britain and Ireland* (London, Aslib, 1953- , issued annually) (Fig. 10).
Some 6000 dissertations are listed in each volume of this work, of which
some 1500 are for the social sciences. It is arranged only in broad subject
groups, such as economics, and political science, each of which is further
subdivided, although even so it can be extremely time-consuming to search
for all theses on a specific subject. A useful feature is the guide to individual

1501. LYONS, H. **(O)** A structural analysis of the symbolism of the Kabblah. B.Litt.
1502. MARTINEZ-ALIER, V. **(O)** Marriage, class and colour in nineteenth-century Cuba. D.Phil.
1503. O'TOOLE, J. J. **(O)** Watts and Woodstock, family and politics among American Negroes and Cape Coloureds. D.Phil.
1504. RYAN, P. M. **(O)** A preliminary inquiry into Hausa symbolism. B.Litt.
1505. SCHUYLER JONES **(O)** Kalashum political organization: a study of village government in Waigal Valley, Nuristan. D.Phil.
1506. TONKIN, J. E. A. **(O)** Some aspects of language from the viewpoint of social anthropology, with particular reference to multilingual situations in Nigeria. D.Phil.
1507. WILLSON-PEPPER, C. R. **(O)** Office in Arabian Bedouin societies. B.Litt.
1507a. BARRETT, S. R. **(Sx)** God's kingdom on stilts: a comparative study of rapid economic development. D.Phil.
1508. REDCLIFT, M. R. **(Sx)** Social change and community in Gema. D.Phil.

Sociology

See also Educational Sociology, p. 53; Social Anthropology, p. 65; Industrial Sociology, p. 90; Social and Industrial Medicine, p. 232

1509. BRANCH, G. M. **(Ab)** Pentecostalism as a deviant medical system. M.Litt.
1510. BARHOUM, M. I. **(B)** Sociological time series and its application to the study of suicide. Ph.D.
1511. BELLAMY, P. C. W. **(B)** Family care and mental illness—a study of needs and services. M.A.
1512. RAPSTOFF, C. I. **(B)** Variables to motivation: value and attitude related to social class differentials in educational attainment. M.Soc.Sc.
1513. BENTLEY, S. **(Brad)** The structure of leadership among Indians, Pakistanis and West Indians in Britain. M.Sc.
1514. BROWN, M. J. **(Brad)** An analysis of probation service practice. Ph.D.
1515. LONGDEN, W. **(Brad)** City of Bradford police: a study in the sociology of organisations. M.Sc.
1516. THOMPSON, J. C. **(Brad)** The referral process in child guidance. Ph.D.
1517. GILES, H. **(Bri)** A study of speech patterns in social interaction: accent evaluation and accent change. Ph.D.
1518. FRAIN, J. P. A. **(Bru)** The changing function of the newspaper. M.Tech.
1519. HAWKINS, K. O. **(C)** Parole selection: the American experience. Ph.D.
1520. NATH, J. **(D)** Some aspects of the life of Indians and Pakistanis in Newcastle, with special reference to women. M.A.
1521. BAYNES, J. C. M. **(E)** The British army in modern society. M.Sc.

Fig. 10. *Index to Theses. . . .* (Reproduced by permission of Aslib.)

universities' regulations as to the availability of theses, as this varies from one to five years at different institutions. Unfortunately for those wanting current information, the work is presently running some four years out of date.

The equivalent source of information for American and Canadian theses is contained in a series of works, issued by University Micro-films at Ann Arbor, Michigan. The major part of the series is *Dissertation Abstracts International* (1969- , issued monthly) (Figs. 11A and 11B), which replaced *Dissertation Abstracts* which appeared between 1952 and 1969 and which was preceded by *Microfilm Abstracts,* which ran from 1938 to 1951. The abstracts in the current work are quite detailed, but they are limited to those works which are available for sale on microfilm or in a full-size copy, and not all universities permit this. However, as a guide to what can be seen with the minimum of difficulty, it is particularly useful, although again the broad subject headings make searching time-consuming, not to say tedious, as the keywork index does not necessarily reveal all items on a specific subject. A comprehensive list of all theses is *American Doctoral Dissertations* (1957- , issued annually), which is arranged by broad subject headings and subdivided by name of the awarding university. No abstracts are given in this work, which is the successor to *Doctoral Dissertations Accepted by American Universities* (New York, Wilson, 1934- , issued annually). The final work in the University Microfilm series is *Masters' Abstracts: abstracts of selected Masters' theses on microfilm* (1964- , issued quarterly).

Some journals contain lists of doctoral theses in their subject field. One of the most notable is *American Economic Review* (Washington, American Economic Association, 1911- , issued quarterly), which in the September issue of each year publishes a list of completed theses, giving abstracts for approximately half the entries. *American Political Science Review* (Washington, American Political Science Association, 1906- , issued quarterly) until 1967 included an annual section of "Doctoral dissertations in political science in the universities of the United States and Canada", the first part of which was particularly useful because it was one of the few sources of information on theses in progress. Its function has now been taken over, but excluding the Canadian universities, by *PS Newsletter of the American Political Science Association* (Washington, The Association, 1968- , issued bi-monthly). Sociology is covered in a similar way by *American Journal of Sociology* (University of Chicago Press, 1898- , issued bi-monthly), which annually lists all higher degrees conferred in the year in universities of the United States and Canada, as well as doctoral dissertations in progress in those countries.

TABLE OF CONTENTS

The Table of Contents lists in alphabetical order the principal subject categories of the dissertations abstracted. For the convenience of readers a Keyword Title Index and Author Index is included following the abstracts.

Fig. 11A. *Dissertation Abstracts International.* (Reproduced by permission of University Microfilms.)

POLITICAL SCIENCE

POLITICAL SCIENCE, GENERAL

POLITICAL CENTRALIZATION IN THE FEDERALISM OF THE UNITED STATES

William Paul ALEXANDER, JR., Ph.D.
The University of Rochester, 1973

This essay clarifies a question concerning federalism in the United States about which there has been considerable confusion. That question concerns the extent of centralization which has occurred within the American federal system since its inception. A distinction is made between administrative centralization and political centralization. This is an important distinction because administrative decisions are largely shaped by political influences.

Our study shows, by means of a time series presenting the federal proportion of domestic governmental expenditures (the expenditures of federal, state and local governments) that between 1840 and 1962 the national government's proportion of all expenditures has risen from about one-sixth to about one-half. Acting on the assumption that expenditures can be approximately equated with administrative activity, an assumption which is corroborated by other evidence introduced in the study, we conclude that administrative centralization has occurred on about the same scale.

To decide whether or not political centralization has occurred in the federalism of the United States and by how much it is necessary to discover the actual location of the authority to make public policy. The political decision-makers in the United States are the political party leaders. The degree of centralization and decentralization in the system as a whole depends on the extent to which the political parties are centralized. If they are centralized so is the constitutional system. If they are not, neither is the constitutional system.

To discover whether or not there had been any political centralization in the federalism of the United States, William H. Riker's disharmony index was computed by bienniums for an 132 year time series from 1837 to 1969. The disharmony index, though it swings widely in the period 1837-1969, does not swing in any consistent direction. A trend line fitted to the series by the least squares methods shows an insignificant negative slope of .0008. Our conclusion is that the basic political structure of American federalism has remained substantially unchanged since 1837.

Order No. 73-25,788, 161 pages.

POLITICAL DEVELOPMENT AND POLITICAL DECAY IN INTERWAR GREECE

Paul Michael ANGELIDES, Ph.D.
The Ohio State University, 1973

Adviser: Professor Louis Nemzer

The basic problem dealt with in this study is the rise of authoritarian dictatorship in the context of modernization. The inquiry focuses on the nature of the process of transition tradition to modernity and the mechanisms of change. Wh any, is the historical role of authoritarianism in a moderr ing setting? What is the conceptual-analytical perspectiv that would render such a role meaningful and amenable to further--and much needed--systematic analysis?

As the scope and intensity of change affect different s sectors differently, a modernizing society requires a min of stability and coordination, particularly among the polit elites--lest continuity is lost and processes of change be estranged from basic and deeply-rooted referents of soci political utility and meaningfulness. In some cases, wher traditional patterns survive and adjust to accommodate th initial "wave" of modernization, key features of the socia structure and cultural system provide for such minimal bility by channeling role and structure differentiation alo pre-existing, institutionalized patterns of social action. I under certain conditions of rapid and uneven modernizati affecting the very core of the social structure by providir ternative patterns, continuity is broken, existing patterns social action become dysfunctional, and stability is under and ultimately lost thus confronting the system with pros of disintegration and breakdown.

The transition process is seen here as consisting c number of interrelated but distinct phases. The phase se is not normally smooth or uniform, and while socio-econ modernization may affect unidirectional and irreversible in some societal sectors, the overall process is reversib meet the needs of balanced modernization and system sta Rapid social mobilization and economic development brin modernization but not political development. The key tes the latter is the ability of a polity to meet the multiple ch lenges and destabilizing effects of the former. The thrus rapid modernization, given direction by certain moderniz "agents," leads a society into what has been called the th point of political development, a juncture at which the eff of mobilization and differentiation (e.g., new social and e nomic groupings, new political alignments and organizati etc.), make it imperative that these are incorporated by polity into an ongoing structure of authority, legitimacy, hierarchy and resource allocation. Failure in a polity's pacity to affect this results in system breakdown and los stability.

Hence the view of political development as a dialectic lationship between the imperatives of capacity, equality structural differentiation. It is herein, in the on-going c frontation and conflict between different sectors of the s) and their respective demands and priorities, that both th promise and the challenge of sustained modernization an litical development lie. If, as in the case of Greece, the is unable to satisfy the new demands and the integrative identific requirements of new social groups and organiza instability and system breakdown follow, and the priority covert to the requirements for system stability and socia ance.

In this setting, some authoritarian regimes, by virtue their strategic position of power and resource accessibil may perform a role of system stabilizer and hence provi an important segment of the groundwork (e.g., adjudicati social legislation, capital accumulation and outlays, the f tions of socialization and national integration, etc.), for fi growth and development. Thus in some cases of unev

---

Fig. 11B. *Dissertation Abstracts International.* (Reproduced by permission of University Microfilms.)

SURVEY ARCHIVES

A wealth of information is collected in surveys conducted by governments, market research and public-opinion organizations, academic and research bodies on all aspects of economic, political, and social life, but much of this information is never published in book or report form. Nonetheless, this information can supplement data available in published statistics, and it can provide useful comparison with any survey being carried out by a researcher.

Survey archives or data banks which store information are a relatively recent innovation. Their creation was made possible by the developments in computer technology, which allows coded information to be stored and later disseminated at high speed. Such archives exist to make data already collected and susceptible of machine analysis available to other researchers for secondary analysis.

Secondary analysis is valuable for several reasons. Firstly, surveys are not only very time-consuming to produce but they are also extremely expensive. Thus if a survey on some subject has already been conducted, it is far more economical to rely on that data. Ralph L. Bisco, in *Data Bases, Computers and the Social Sciences* (New York, Wiley, 1970), has shown that the cost of acquiring information from data banks can be as little as one fifteen-thousandth of the cost of a new data-collecting operation. Secondly, much information collected in surveys never appears in the reports which result from the exercise, as many questions of a basic kind, especially of a demographic nature, are included only as background, but as surveys are deposited in the archives in their entirety, all information is available for use by other researchers. Thus it is possible for researchers using secondary analysis to have access to all surveys which include a question on a particular topic, even where such a question was not of very great importance in some of the original surveys, thereby covering a wider population than it might otherwise have been feasible to do if he were conducting his own survey. Similarly, time-lapse and ecological comparisons become possible with far greater speed and at far less financial cost than they would be otherwise.

The major British data bank for social scientists is the SSRC Survey Archive, which is maintained at the University of Essex, in Colchester. This archive was established in 1967, and collects data relating to social and economic affairs from academic, commercial, and government sources, so as to make this information available for further analysis. Thus data collected by, for example, a market research organization, may be analysed by a researcher with an entirely different purpose, who may be studying poverty or demographic characteristics. To enable subscribers to have easy access to information regarding what is available, the Survey Archive issues several guides to its holdings. These include descriptions of materials relating to particular subjects or special collections, details about the contents of individual sets of data, and a general catalogue which is regularly up-dated with supplements. The general catalogue and its supplements are in the form of a KWIC index, in which the original text, or in some cases a paraphrase, of each question appears in order of each keyword in it. Hence a question including four significant words would have four entries in the index. A detailed *Enquirers Handbook* is also issued, giving full instructions on how to use the several guides to the Archive's contents.

A rather more specialized archive is the Central Register of Business, which is maintained by the Office of Business Statistics at the Department of Trade and Industry. This, as its name implies, is devoted to business information, and it is useful because it up-dates published statistics and allows them to be used more easily in different ways. Another specialized archive is the demand driven file on British political history at the University of Strathclyde in Glasgow. This is a collection of election results since 1885 together with biographical information on twentieth-century Members of Parliament.

In the United States there are very many data banks housing survey information — so many in fact that it becomes problematic for the researcher to know which can most satisfactorily satisfy his needs. The Council of Social Science Data Archives at the University of Pittsburgh, Pennsylvania 15213, publishes a register of American data bases and gives details of new ones being established in its bulletin, *News and Notes* (Pittsburgh, the Council, 1966- , issued irregularly). The Center for the Advancement of Library-Information Science, University Graduate Division, City University of New York, has issued an international directory, *Data Bases in the Social and Behavioral Sciences* (New York, Science Associates, 1972), which aims to solve the problem of locating and assessing data banks.

A major archive is the Roper Public Opinion Research Center at Williams College, Williamstown, Massachusetts. The archive was established in 1946 and now holds some 7500 studies covering politics, economics and business, education, health and welfare, occupations and professions, mass communications, public opinion, organizations, community problems, inter-group relations, and other social science topics, both for the United States and for over forty other countries. Universities such as Yale, UCLA, Michigan State, and Illinois, as well as Massachusetts Institute of Technology, maintain their own data banks, and so too do government departments such as the Bureau of Labor Statistics, and new bases are constantly being developed. It should be possible for any interested researcher, even with only limited funds, to gain access to this wealth of data with no difficulty.

As mentioned in Chapter 2, there is a great deal of ephemeral and primary material which is of potential value to researchers, much of which is available, though not well documented, in libraries. It has been hoped for some time that the British Library will be able to improve the guides to such material, but meanwhile there is a service of limited subject scope but maximum impact. Its title is *Harvester Primary Social Sources* (Brighton, Sussex, 1973-). It covers material relating to Britain and European integration issued by sixty-nine British pressure groups since 1945. Much of this material has never been available in libraries, since at the time of its publication it was not regarded as being of very great significance. The service's main collection is on microfiche, and it is equipped with detailed indexes.

Much other ephemeral or primary material can be found in local history libraries of the public library system, but the quality of the collections varies considerably from area to area. The best house all the material which has been published relating to the area, together with all material by or about local inhabitants, and have good collections of local newspapers, school and church magazines, records of local societies and industrial firms or businesses, playbills, and a wealth of other material. These can clearly be of great value to a researcher interested in historical aspects of his subject.

CHAPTER 9

Social Administration

Because social administrators rely to a great extent on material aimed primarily at academic social scientists, much of the information given in the previous chapters will be of potential value to them, but for the sake of brevity it will not be repeated here. Thus each section of this chapter will be devoted to those items which are designed for applied workers, and readers are referred to the preceding chapters for general discussion on the values of particular forms of materials.

Although social administration is generally considered to be primarily the local or national government's responsibility, its scope here will be extended to cover voluntary as well as statutory services, and is aimed at anyone who is concerned with social or economic problems in the widest sense.

CAREERS, TRAINING, AND EMPLOYMENT

Apart from the general guides to careers and training listed in Chapter 1, there are several sources of information relating to social administration and social work. The Social Work Advisory Centre, 26 Bedford Square, London, WC 1, issues a guide to careers and provides information on courses offered by local authorities and universities, giving details as to pre-requisite experience, residential requirements (the probation service, for example, demands that students should spend three weeks in residence in a prison; some courses demand similar periods of residence in a suitable institution such as a children's home). Useful guides to careers are K. Gay's *Careers in Social Service* (New York, Messner, 1969) and *Careers in Counseling and Guidance* by S. C. Stone and B. Shertzer (Boston, Mass., Houghton Mifflin, 1971). The *International Directory of Schools of Social Work* (New York, United Nations, 1955) was useful for its wide coverage, but has unfortunately not been updated.

Sources of information on employment are provided in the general journals and newspapers listed in Chapter 1, and especially in *New Society*. Many of the journals listed below under the heading Books and Periodicals are also useful sources of information on vacancies.

ASSOCIATIONS

Associations in applied social science can be broadly divided into those which cater for the needs and interests of professional workers and those which directly serve people who are in need of assistance.

Details of British associations can be found in the works listed in Chapter 4. A more detailed work, which is especially useful for its depth treatment of the kinds of association which can be approached with specific types of inquiry, such as adoption, alcoholism, physically handicapped, etc., is Phyllis Willmott's *Consumer's Guide to the British Social Services* (Harmondsworth, Middx., Penguin, 3rd edn., 1972). This handbook gives details of the kind of work done by the specialist voluntary bodies as well as of the statutory services which are provided by the local authorities. It is particularly useful for the layman who may be uncertain where to turn for advice on a particular problem. *Social Services Yearbook* (London, Councils of Education Press, 1972-) also aims at covering the whole of the UK services, whether statutory or voluntary. It contains a useful digest of statistics, and for this reason it is of more value to the professional worker than is Wilmott's work. The National Council of Social Service also issues a guide, *Voluntary Social Service* (London, NCSS, 2nd edn., 1973).

Much information on organizations which give assistance is available from the Citizens' Advice Bureaux, which have details of local voluntary agencies which exist for this purpose, many of which are not listed in the published directories because they operate only on a limited basis or because they have only been recently established. Such services include free legal advice and psychiatric counselling, although in some cases a nominal charge may be made to cover the agency's accommodation rental costs. These organizations are usually staffed by professional workers who give their services free of charge, and they are particularly useful for those who are unable to afford a private consultation or who are unable to wait for the often lengthy period before they can be seen at a hospital.

A useful guide to the American bodies is the *Encyclopedia of Social Work* (New York, National Association of Social Workers, 1965- , issued annually). This work includes a detailed directory of American, Canadian, and

International organizations in the field. Another helpful work is the *Public Welfare Directory* (Chicago, American Public Welfare Association, 1940- , issued annually). This is particularly useful because it gives details of each State's administration of public welfare and of where to write for information or assistance regarding specific problems such as mental health, civil rights, ageing, etc. Voluntary social service organizations in the United States are listed in *National Directory of Private Social Agencies* (Flushing, NY, Social Service Publications). This loose-leaf guide lists some 5000 welfare bodies which either give direct assistance to individual applicants or refer them to the proper address. Monthly amendments keep the work up to date.

The following list of organizations of potential interest to applied social scientists is not intended as a comprehensive guide, nor does it aim to list the most important bodies. Its purpose is only to give examples of the kinds of organizations which exist and the kinds of work which is done.

United Kingdom

ASSOCIATION OF FAMILY CASEWORKERS, Oxford House, Derbyshire Street, London, E 2.

ASSOCIATION OF PSYCHIATRIC SOCIAL WORKERS, Oxford House, Derbyshire Street, London, E 2.

BRITISH COUNCIL FOR REHABILITATION OF THE DISABLED, Tavistock House South, Tavistock Square, London, WC1 9LB.

BRITISH RED CROSS SOCIETY, 9 Grosvenor Crescent, London, SW 1. This body provides a wide range of services including nursing, provision of medical equipment for domiciliary patients, ambulance services for the handicapped, and homes for the disabled. It also has a missing-persons bureau. Specific services vary from area to area.

COMMUNITY SERVICE VOLUNTEERS, 28 Commercial Street, London, E 1.

FAMILY SERVICE UNITS, 207 Marylebone Road, London, NW 1. Like the body above, this is a nationwide network of local associations. It provides support for needy families and holidays for children of such families.

HOWARD LEAGUE FOR PENAL REFORM AND HOWARD CENTRE OF PENOLOGY, 125 Kennington Park Road, London, SE 11. This research body issues bibliographies, maintains a substantial library, and publishes an annual review of progress.

INSTITUTE OF RACE RELATIONS, 36 Jermyn Street, London, W 1. This research organization has an excellent library, produces journals and reports of its work as well as bibliographies based on its library's holdings.

NATIONAL COUNCIL FOR CIVIL LIBERTIES, 152 Camden High Street, London, NW 1. The Council produces a number of leaflets on human rights in general, and has issued a guide to women's rights and to the rights of minority groups. It provides legal assistance and advice for its members.

NATIONAL COUNCIL OF SOCIAL SERVICE, 26 Bedford Square, London, WC 1. This is the national co-ordinating body of local councils of social service and of many other organizations. It issues a wide range of publications on both statutory and voluntary social services.

NATIONAL COUNCIL OF VOLUNTARY CHILD CARE ORGANIZA-TIONS, 35 Highbury Park, London, N 5 .

NATIONAL MARRIAGE GUIDANCE COUNCIL, 58 Queen Anne Street, London, W1M 0BT.

NATIONAL SOCIETY FOR MENTALLY HANDICAPPED CHILDREN, 86, Newman Street, London, W1P 4AR.

NATIONAL SOCIETY FOR THE PREVENTION OF CRUELTY TO CHILDREN, 1 Riding House Street, London, W1 P.

NATIONAL SOCIETY OF CHILDREN'S NURSERIES, 45 Russell Square, London, WC 1.

ROYAL NATIONAL INSTITUTE FOR THE BLIND, 224-8 Great Portland Street, London, W1N 6AA.

ROYAL NATIONAL INSTITUTE FOR THE DEAF, 105 Gower Street, London, WC 1.

SPASTICS SOCIETY, 12 Park Crescent, London, W1N 4EQ.

United States

AMERICAN FOUNDATION FOR THE BLIND, 15 West 16th Street, New York, NY 10011. This body provides books for the blind, training and a wide range of welfare services. It also carries out research and maintains a library.

AMERICAN INSTITUTE OF FAMILY RELATIONS, 5287 Sunset Boulevard, Los Angeles, Cal. 90027. This body provides a counselling service and has branches throughout the country.

AMERICAN MENTAL HEALTH FOUNDATION, 2 East 86th Street, New York, NY 10028, is a research body.

ASSOCIATION OF MENTAL HEALTH ADMINISTRATORS, 2901 Lafayette Avenue, Lansing, Mich. 48906.

CONGRESS OF RACIAL EQUALITY, 200 West 135th Street, New York, NY 10030.

JOHN HOWARD ASSOCIATION, 537 South Dearborn Street, Chicago, Ill. 60605. Like its British counterpart this body is concerned with penal reform and is basically a research organization.

NATIONAL ASSOCIATION OF THE DEAF, 814 Thayer Avenue, Silver Spring, Maryland, 20910. This body conducts research, provides schools, and issues a wide range of publications.

NATIONAL ASSOCIATION OF SOCIAL WORKERS, 2 Park Avenue, New York, NY 10016. This is the United States equivalent of the National Council of Social Service in Great Britain.

NATIONAL COMMITTEE FOR CHILDREN AND YOUTH, 1401 K Street, NW Washington, DC 20005. The NCCY serves as the central source of information on all matters concerning children and young people.

NATIONAL COUNCIL ON CRIME AND DELINQUENCY, Continental Plaza, 411 Hackensack Avenue, Hackensack, NJ 07601.

NATIONAL COUNCIL ON FAMILY RELATIONS, 1219 University Avenue, SE Minneapolis, Minn. 55414. The NCFR is a research organization which is active in the field of publishing and issues bibliographies as well as several journals.

NATIONAL COUNCIL ON THE AGING, 1828 L Street, NW Washington, DC 20036. This research organization issues several publications, has a large library and maintains the National Institute of Senior Centers.

NATIONAL EMERGENCY CIVIL LIBERTIES COMMITTEE, 25 East 26th Street, New York, NY 10010.

BOOKS AND PERIODICALS

Many of the general bibliographies listed in Chapter 4 are valuable sources of information on current output in the field of applied social sciences, but a great deal of material, especially where it is of slight size, albeit of significant content, is excluded from such tools. A large amount of pamphlet material is issued by specialist organizations, much of which is overlooked if the more specialized bibliographical tools are not consulted.

Several of the bodies catering for the needs of particular specialists or which carry out their own research, maintain libraries not only of their own publications but also of material issued by other organizations working in the same field. Most such libraries do not publish catalogues, but many are prepared to answer inquiries relating to literature on their specific subject. Institutions which have large libraries include the Institute of Race Relations, which issues bibliographies from time to time; the Tavistock Institute of

Human Relations, whose library covers subjects relating to all aspects of psychology, social psychology, and social problems; and the Howard League for Penal Reform.

Guides to current literature on the applied social sciences tend to be limited to specific fields, but many of the social science bibliographies, indexing, and abstracting services listed in chapters 4 and 5 can be useful. The most general guide devoted to this area is *Abstracts for Social Workers* (Albany, NY, National Association of Social Workers, 1964- , issued quarterly), which provides information on social work and related topics. It has a classified arrangement with author and subject indexes. Most of the material listed in this service is of American origin. A very useful service of more restricted subject scope is *Poverty and Human Resources Abstracts* (Beverly Hills, Sage, 1966- , issued bi-monthly), which is published under the auspices of the Institute of Labor and Industrial Relations. Books, journals, reports, and pamphlets fall into the scope of the work, which is again strongly oriented to American publications.

The most comprehensive British service is *Current Literature on Community Health and Personal Social Service* (London, Department of Health and Social Security, 1972- issued monthly). This is an annotated list based largely on information supplied by local authorities and on materials in the DHSS library. A further useful British work is the *Bibliography of Social and Public Administration* (London, Joint University Council for Social and Public Administration, 1954), which is a basic classified listing of selected articles from British journals from 1930 to 1952, and is up-dated by annual supplements.

More specialized services include:

Abstracts on Criminology and Penology (Amsterdam, Holland, Excerpta Criminological Foundation, 1961- , issued bi-monthly).

Child Development Abstracts and Bibliography (Lafayette, Ind., Purdue University Society for Research in Child Development, 1927- , issued three times yearly).

Crime and Delinquency Abstracts (Bethesda, Maryland, National Council on Crime and Delinquency, 1963- , issued eight times yearly), has retrospective coverage to 1961.

DSH Abstracts (Washington, American Speech and Hearing Association, 1960- , issued quarterly).

Hospital Abstracts (London, HMSO, 1961- , issued monthly). This work covers all but the medical and related professional aspects of hospitals and their administration.

Index to Current' Hospital Literature (Washington, American Hospital Association, 1945- , issued semi-annually with quinquennial cumulations).

International Bibliography of Studies on Alcohol (New Brunswick, NJ, Rutgers Center of Alcohol Studies, 1966- , issued annually).

Social Security Abstracts (Geneva, International Social Security Association, 1963- , issued quarterly) is based on the entries which appear in *World Bibliography of Social Security* (Geneva, International Social Security Association, 1962- , issued quarterly). The scope of this and the above series is wider than that implied by their titles, and extends to social services in general, social work, and social medicine.

There are many retrospective bibliographies of potential use to those working in the applied social science fields of which the following titles are given merely as examples of the kinds of works available. *Disaffiliated Man: essays and bibliography on skid row, vagrancy and outsiders,* edited by Howard M. Baker (University of Toronto Press, 1971). This work contains an extensively annotated two-hundred-page bibliography of books and journal articles covering skid row and its men, taverns and bars, the law, alcoholism, employment and unemployment, voluntary associations, aging and disaffiliation, anomie, isolation, and marginality. The work is equipped with a detailed subject index. The *Sociology and Anthropology of Mental Illnesss* by Edwin D. Driver (Amherst, University of Massachusetts Press, 1965) aims to cover the literature of the treatment, social, and cultural aspects of mental illness throughout the world, and the *International Bibliography of Research in Marriage and the Family, 1900-1964* by Joan Aldous and Reuben Hill (University of Minnesota Press for the Minnesota Family Study Center and the Institute of Life Insurance, 1967) is a keyword in context index of almost 13,000 items in books, journals, and fugitive materials, mostly in English, but with just over 10 per cent of the material listed being in other languages. What promises to be a useful guide is *The Use of Criminological Literature,* edited by Martin Wright (London, Butterworths, 1974). The work is aimed at academic social scientists, practising social workers, and others with an interest in criminology. It will cover sociological, psychiatric, and legal aspects of the subject.

Periodicals can be traced in the sources listed in Chapter 5, but the following are examples of some of the more commonly available titles:

Applied Social Studies: an international journal of social work education, administration and research (Oxford, Pergamon, 1969- , issued three times yearly).

British Journal of Psychiatric Social Work (London, Association of Psychiatric Social Workers, 1947- , issued semi-annually).

Case Conference: a professional journal for the social worker and social administrator (Croydon, Association of Social Workers and Case Conference, 1954- , issued monthly).

Child Care (London, National Council of Voluntary Child Care Organizations, 1947- , issued quarterly).

Howard Journal of Penology and Crime Prevention (London, Howard League, 1946- , issued annually).

International Social Worker (Bombay, India, International Council on Social Welfare, International Association of Schools of Social Work, and the International Federation of Social Workers, 1958- , issued quarterly).

Journal of Rehabilitation (Washington, National Rehabilitation Association, 1935- , issued bi-monthly).

Journal of Marriage and the Family (Minneapolis, National Council on Family Relations, 1938- , issued quarterly).

New Society (London, New Science Publications, 1962- , issued weekly).

Race (London, Institute of Race Relations, 1959- , issued quarterly).

Social Casework (Washington, Family Service Association of America, 1920- , issued monthly).

Social Service Quarterly (London, National Council of Social Service, 1947-).

Social Service Review: devoted to the scientific and professional interests of social work (University of Chicago Press, 1927- , issued quarterly).

Social Work (London, Association of Family Caseworkers, 1944- , issued quarterly).

Social Work (New York, National Association of Social Workers, 1956- , issued quarterly).

The majority of the journals listed above are indexed or abstracted in the sources mentioned in Chapter 5. *Psychological Abstracts* (Washington, American Psychological Association, 1927- , issued monthly) is particularly useful as a guide to recent journal coverage of specific topics.

Some social workers will undoubtedly find it useful to be aware of these journals which, while not being designed with them in mind, contain valuable insights into the societies with which they are concerned. The best guide to such titles is *The Directory of Alternative Media Periodicals* (Brighton,

Smoothie, 2nd., 1972), which lists many journals which cannot be located in the more traditional sources, e.g. *Simon Star,* the newsletter of the Simon Community, and *Grassroots.*

There are no separate sources of information on government publications: those who are interested in this type of material are referred to Chapter 6.

Apart from the directories mentioned earlier in this chapter under the heading Associations, there are few reference works devoted to social work and applied social sciences. The major encyclopedia is the *Encyclopedia of Social Work* mentioned above, which covers the historical development of the subject as well as current problems. There are no really up-to-date monolingual dictionaries apart from *Dictionary of Social Services: policy and practice,* edited by Joan Clegg (London, National Council of Social Service, 1972). The most useful translating dictionary is *Wörterbuch der Sozialarbeit,* edited by K. Zapf (Cologne, Haymanns-Verlag, 1961), which contains some 5000 German words with indexes in English, Dutch, French, Italian, and Spanish. Many of the other works listed in Chapter 7 contain useful information for those in the field of social administration.

Research in progress is listed in the guides noted in Chapter 8, but there are also some guides which are devoted specifically to narrower subjects, as, for example, *Research Relating to Children* (Washington, USGPO, 1950- , issued annually). The first volume of this series covered work which was started or completed during the period from December 1948 to June 1949. Each issue is arranged by broad subjects, and abstracts of the research papers are included. Another guide is *Old Age: a register of social research* (London, National Corporation for the Care of Old People, 1964). Although it has not been up-dated, the Corporation does maintain a list of current work, as do many of the research and professional associations listed above. Completed theses are abstracted each year in the September issue of *Social Service Review* under the heading Doctoral Dissertations in Social Work, but the list is limited to those works which are submitted to graduate schools of social work. Other theses can be located in the dissertations lists noted in Chapter 8.

APPENDIX

Report on a Literature Search for Information Regarding the Effect of the Imprisonment of Either Parent on the Family

This appendix has been included to show the way in which a detailed literature search on a specific subject can be carried out, and to illustrate the kinds of problem which can be encountered.

Profile: the work was undertaken for a social worker who was to undertake a special study on the topic.

Types of material to be included: American and British books, journal articles and theses, British reports, and current research projects, from 1960 to date. British newspaper articles from *The Times* and the *Guardian* were to be included for their informational value, the portrayal of current social values and attitudes, and — in retrospect — social change, and to enable as exhaustive an approach as possible to be made, as little has been written on the subject.

Subject orientation and possible entry terms into the bibliographical services: None of the standard dictionaries yielded any suitable terms, so a standard book on the subject, *Prisoners and their Families* by P. J. Morris (London, Allen & Unwin, 1965), was checked to see what terms were given large numbers of index entries. A list of possible entry terms was compiled which included "women", "wives", "mothers", "fathers", "fatherless families", "family", "problem family", "delinquent family", "family social work", "child(ren)", "prison(er-s)", "rehabilitation", and "parents", to which likely synonymous were added, such as "crime and criminals", "one-parent families", "after care", and "social problems".

THE SEARCH FOR BOOKS

British National Bibliography

Search terms: yielded the following classification marks as possible entry points: 301.42 — family; 301.43 — children; 361 — welfare work; 362.8 — welfare services for families, unmarried mothers, minority groups; 364 — criminology; 364.8 — criminology, after-care; 365.66 — welfare for prisoners.

The search under all these entry points from the cumulative volumes from 1960 revealed one book — that already mentioned, by P. J. Morris, under the class mark 365.661.

Whitaker's Cumulative Book List

Search terms: the arrangement of this work being primarily by authors and title key words, with only a very broad subject approach meant that it was necessary to rely on one of the search terms being included in a title. The only entry duplicated that of *BNB*.

Cumulative Book Index

Search terms: "prisoners" and "family" gave references to "rehabilitation of criminals", "social work with delinquents", and "criminals", which widened the field.

The information yielded was greater in volume than in any of the above services, but all the works retrieved appeared to be too general for the purpose of the list being compiled. Morris's book was again mentioned.

International Bibliography of Sociology

Search terms: yielded the following classification marks which appeared to be of possible value: marriage and family C6; family and kinship C63; social problems: crime and delinquency F15; punishment and penal institutions F16; social work and social service F22.

The classification thought most likely to be fruitful was F15, but in fact F16 revealed two items during the period of the search, Morris's book, and one which it was thought was too general to be of great significance.

London Bibliography of the Social Sciences

Search terms: "prisoners", and "families", yielded several references, including one to "prisoners' families", which resulted in the book by Morris being located yet again.

Comments

The subject heading approach seemed to be easier and less time-consuming than did the classified arrangement, as the schemes used in *BNB* and *IBS* did not cater adequately for this subject in that there were several possible places where it could have been located. The *LBSS* listed ninety-two titles under "prisoners" but had a detailed sub-arrangement in which only three titles appeared under a possibly useful (and in this instance actually useful) heading, whereas the arrangement of *IBS* had in one issue twenty-one entries under F16, in author order, all of which had to be checked to see whether they were appropriate.

One useful book was not retrieved from the search in the usual tools, that by J. P. Martin, entitled *The Social Consequences of Conviction, 1958-70,* which was published in 1971, and located through the Home Office *Summary of Research in Progress and of Research Supported by Grant,* which stated in its abstract of that work that it covered prisoners' families, employment, rehabilitation, etc. There might well have been other works, which because of the vagueness of their titles, or because they included only one or two chapters on the subject of the search had been overlooked.

THE SEARCH FOR PERIODICAL AND NEWSPAPER ARTICLES

British Humanities Index
Search terms: the initial terms yielded references giving a total of fourteen headings to be searched. The most useful were all located under the heading "prisoners" with subdivisions "after-care", "children of", "families", "wives of", and from the start of the period under examination yielded a total of five items, with a further four under the headings: "men, married, in prison"; "mothers, in prison".

Social Sciences and Humanities Index
Search terms: twelve terms were used in total, but only one item was revealed. It was, however, one which had not been listed in *BHI.*

The Index to The Times
Search terms: "family", "children", "rehabilitation", and "prisoners" were used. "Crime", rather than "prisoners", was the term used in the index from 1960 to 1964. From 1966 to 1971 six potentially useful items were traced, as well as two which were considered too ephemeral for inclusion in the list. "Crime" supplied two items in the period 1961-64, and the term "children" revealed another item appearing in 1970.

Sociological Abstracts
Search terms: "prison(er-s)", "rehabilitation", "family", "child(ren)". The keyword index which appeared at the end of each year was used. The term

"prisoners" resulted in one item classified in the "social disorganization" section in 1962, and "children" yielded another item under "family and socialization of children" in August 1972.

Psychological Abstracts

Search terms: "crime and criminals", "prison", "prison inmates" and "rehabilitation". "Prison" provided two items in 1968 and 1969, "crime and criminals" one item in 1971, all of which appeared in the broad section "clinical psychology – crime".

Current Contents

It was necessary to make the search as current as possible, but the broad subject approach made it a time-consuming task to search through all the weekly parts for three months under the headings "social issues and problems" and "law". Only one item was retrieved from this service, under the heading "social issues and problems".

Individual Journal Indexes

Twenty titles which had been fruitful as a result of checking the general indexing services, or which appeared from their titles, sub-titles, or sponsoring organization to be potentially valuable were checked via their individual annual indexes, these being more detailed than general indexing services and including many items which would be deemed of too little significance for inclusion in the wider services. Details of these journals were obtained from *Ulrich's International Periodicals Directory*. These indexes contributed nothing. Newspaper articles could not be up-dated without checking individual copies; it was decided that this would be too time-consuming to be worthwhile, as items from the *Guardian* would be indexed in *BHI*, and *The Times Index* would appear ultimately – although this is some six to eighteen months out of date, the volume for the previous calendar year appearing in June.

Comments

Four arrangements were encountered: broad subject in *CC;* subject headings in *BHI, SSHI, The Times Index;* a subject index in *PA* and a keyword index in *SA* where a classified arrangement occurs. Many search terms had to be used to cope with the scatter of items under the different headings used in the several services. For example *SSHI*, 16, 1960-2 under the heading "Children – Great Britain", includes an item "Life with Mother", but this entry is not repeated under the heading "Mothers". Uniform sets of headings tend to be used in every volume of a service, regardless of the appropriateness to individual items being indexed, and reliance on references from the term anticipated to the one actually used can be time-consuming and sometimes unsatisfactory. A particular problem is the keyword index arrangement of *SA*, as this is based on words used in the titles of the articles, whereas in searching for literature on a specific subject one is approaching by words suggested by the subject concerned. Unless all possible words and their synonyms are checked, recall of possibly useful items will be low.

The most notable fact about the search for journal articles is that only two items were duplicated in the several services, and *BHII, SSHI* and *PA* covered some 70 per cent of the potentially useful journals between them, whilst 15 per cent of all journals were covered by a combination of any two of these services. More significant is the fact that 20 per cent of potentially useful journals are not indexed by any of these sources, to which the 10 per cent only covered by *CC* could be added, as a retrospective check of this service is not viable.

THE SEARCH FOR THESES

Dissertation Abstracts International: a humanities and social sciences
Search terms: for volumes without an index (1970-2) the sections "social work", "sociology — general", "criminology", "family", and "public welfare" were chosen from the table of contents. In volumes 1966-7, where a keyword index was supplied, the terms "prisoners", "children", "parents", "wives", "mothers", "family", and "father" were used. The abstracts from 1960 to 1966 had subject indexes, and were approached using the terms "prisoners", "family", "father", "mother", "children", and "parents". Four items in total were located.
Index to Theses Accepted for Higher Degrees . . . .
Search terms: the broad sections on "sociology", "law", and "politics — local government: local welfare", and "housing" seemed to be appropriate areas to search. All the entries in these sections were scanned but nothing discovered.

Comments

The keyword index in the later volumes of DAI was time-consuming to search; ITT was very time-consuming also, as the arrangement by broad subject resulted in large numbers of items to check. Conversely, the broad subject arrangement ensures that no items are lost through the unavoidable scatter of subjects and related items inherent in a close classification. Nonetheless, searching through eleven columns in the index under the entry "children" in DAI was as time-sonsuming as it would have been to search through the relevant sections of the text. The lack of up-to-dateness of the British service was a serious drawback.

THE SEARCH FOR REPORTS

BLL Announcement Bulletin

The broad heading "behavioural and social sciences and humanities" resulted in the search through this service being tedious, the average number of entries in any one issue under that heading being 50. Only one work other than one found in BNB was located.

BRITISH RESEARCH IN PROGRESS

Home Office Research and Statistics Department: Summary of Research in Progress . . .

Search terms: the headings "custodial treatment", "crime and criminals", seemed to be the most potentially useful. Two items of value were discovered, neither of which had been located in previously examined sources, although each had been published by 1972.

Scientific Research in British Universities and Colleges, V3

Search terms: the subject index was examined using the terms "prisoners", "rehabilitation", "family, and children". The term "prisoners" revealed four items, two of which had been located elsewhere, two of which could not be located anywhere else.

SSRC Newsletter

Search terms: all items had to be read as there is no classified index. One four-year project was listed for the (then) current year.

Comments

Lack of abstracts in all but the Home Office guide made the tools less useful than they could have been.

CONCLUSIONS

The work involved in gathering together a comprehensive list of material on this narrow subject was considerable. Nonetheless, it is necessary to consult a wide variety of sources in an attempt to acquire full coverage. Even so, it is likely that not all the material has been located, but it can fairly safely be assumed that everything of significance has been retrieved.

Index to Authors, Titles and Subjects.

Notes on using the index.

1. Only the first named author of a work by more than one person is indexed.
2. Works issued by organisations described in this book are indexed under the name of the issuing body, with the exception of periodicals, all of which are listed by title.
3. Works for which notes 1 and 2 do not apply are entered under title.
4. Page numbers in italics refer to illustrations.

135